Reflecting On The Morning E Mail

John Ferri

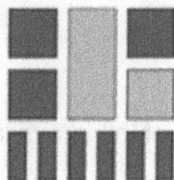

C & L Publishers House
PO Box 2048
Washington D.C. 20013

Published in the United States of America by
C & L Publishers House
Washington D.C.

Ferri, John, 1955-
    Reflecting on the Morning E Mail - 1st ed.
    p.cm.
    ISBN 978-0-692-47361-0 (Soft cover)

Reflecting on the Morning E Mail is available at special dis-
counts.
For more information, please contact the C&L Publishers House,
PO Box 2048, Washington D.C. 20013, or e mail John.Ferri@
CLPubHouse.com. Website: www.CLPubHouse.com

This book is dedicated to
my grandchildren
& to future generations
of
La Bella Verita

Table of Contents

Preface

*T*his book is a list of "Thoughts of the Day" that were sent to my two daughters when they left home to attend college. The "Thoughts of the Day" are morning reflections that are based on events of the day. The events were of family, local, national and international in nature. Even though the "Thoughts of the Day" are based on past events, they can easily apply in today's time and living environment. The time frame of these reflections span five (5) years. Not all of the daily reflections are listed.

The e mail addresses, references and dates have been modified. The dates have been changed to seasons. References have been eliminated. The "From" address is "Poppi" and the "To" address is "La Bella Verita", Italian for "The Beautiful Truth". This is what every child is. All of the e mail's consist of a "Thought of the Day", but a portion also have an introductory sentence or short paragraph added. Credit is given where known. Others are anonymous and others are my own thoughts.

I recently completed a Professional service contract with the US National Aeronautics and Science Administration (NASA). The contract consisted of providing Architectural and Project Management services during the renovation of NASA Headquarters, located on Capitol Hill, Washington D.C. I added NASA related stories to the introduction of certain categories where appropriate. I envoked "Artistic License" on occasion for emphasis.

The original e mails were downloaded into a folder in 2005. The folder was transferred onto a backup external hard drive. I recently came upon the folder when accessing the hard drive for reference reports. That is when the idea for this book started to crystallize. As I reread the e mails I started to place them into categories; lessons in competition, lessons in schoolwork and lessons in "Other" (Values, Family Traditions, Political events, etc.)

7

Recently, I became a Grandfather, and with this status in life, the meaning of this book became more important. This book has now become "Thoughts on Life Lessons" for the next generation. The three categories have been reevaluated and are now "Thoughts" on four parts of Life. Each part dependant upon the previous one.

The first part is" Life is a Journey", which consists of two chapters: Dreams and The Day of Trepidation - September 11, 2001. Everyone has dreams. They give us hope. Our dreams may have to be adjusted as we experience life, but they can never be crushed. We may change the dreams that we chase, but we will always have a dream. Without a dream, we exist and die.

The second chapter is to remind the next generation that Dreams can be derailed by influences that are not under anyone's control. That life is very precious and that at any minute, an uncontrolled event may change or redirect life in a direction that was not anticipated.

The second part is "The Sustenance of Life", which consists of three chapters: Faith, Family and Values. Human beings need the sustenance of food, water and air in order to survive. This part establishes the three key areas of life needed for a person to achieve fulfillment. The days succeeding September 11, 2001, I found a photograph of my sister and my two daughters in front of the World Trade Center Towers. I gave that photo to her on her birthday in October 2001 with the caption "Sustenance of Life: Family, Values and Faith". After deep contemplation, Faith needs to be the   first Sustenance of Life.

The third part is "The Foundation of Fulfillment", which consists of three chapters: Learn, Compete and Create. Learning is the basis for decision making. Learning is more than studying a trade or educational books. You learn by being aware of events of each day. Successful people never stop learning. Competition is the greatest teacher because through competition one learns from both failure and success. One learns to improve or what is needed to improve upon undeveloped areas. Honesty is developed when the competition is with oneself. Being creative is thinking how something can be done differently. It develops confidence in risk taking.

The fourth part of the book is "The Framework for Living", which consists of three chapters: Relationships, Vocation and Freedom. Interacting with people is the most important activity that a person does on a daily basis. Vocation is the decision to enact your Life Plan. Freedom allows you to be successful in implementing your plan.

So, the journey begins with a Dream. Chasing the Dream may be derailed on occasion by unforeseen actions. Faith, Family and Right-Wrong Value judgements keep you on the path to fulfill the Dream. Learn what is needed to act on the Dream. Compete in the arena of ideas. Reevaluate the failures and success of the competition and create your unique path to achieving success. Enjoy healthy relationships along the journey. Choose the vocation that fits within your plan and appreciate the Freedom for the opportunity to fulfill your Dream.

ENJOY

Life is a Journey

Dreams

The Day of
Trepidation
September 11, 2001

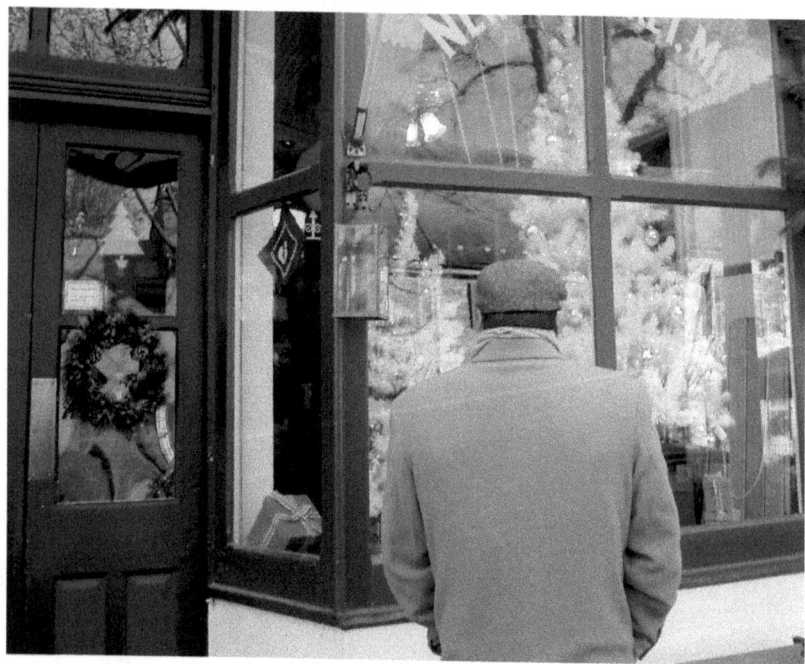

Dreams

Btween 2011 and 2014, I had a contract to provide Design & Project Management Services to NASA for their Headquarters Renovation. NASA is located 1 1/2 blocks from the Smithsonian Air and Space Museum on the National Mall. Tourists usually make a stop into the NASA Headquarters Main Lobby to see artifacts from the various missions that include Space Suits, a Nobel Prize for Chemistry, and gifts from various countries and dignitaries. There is also a live link to the International Space Station to view the daily routine of the astronauts on board. Also open to the public is the NASA Library that houses research, artifacts, models and autographed photographs from different presidents, astronauts. Children that visit the NASA Library are given lectures and outreach items to take home with them.

One day I was verifying Library artifacts for the design program of the renovation project. A group of families were present listening to a NASA Scientist give an enthusiastic lecture on science and technology. One child was blind. The Librarian directed the blind girl to an information board that was in braille. The board explained Astrophysics, the science of the stars and universe, Heliophysics, the science of the sun & Planetary Science, the science of searching for life on other planets.

After the lecture, the librarian asked the children in attendance what they want to be when they grow up. The blind girl answered that she wants to be a NASA Scientist and study what heaven is like. There were some smirks from the small crowd, as how can this blind girl achieve her dream. The NASA Scientist whispered in the little girls ear, "I am going to tell you a secret. You will make a great NASA Scientist, you know Scientists can not see 80% of what they are studying."
BELIEVE IN YOUR DREAM.

From: Poppi
To: La Bella Verita
Sent: Winter

> This weekend is Great-Grand mom's Birthday party. She is 93
> years young. She is the last surviving immigrant.

Thought of the Day:
I arrived by ship to New York as a teenager, an immigrant, and
like millions of others before me, my first sight was the Statue
of Liberty and the amazing skyline of Manhattan. I have NEVER
forgotten that sight or what it stands for.
Daniel Libeskind
Architect/Master Planner of the WTC Revitalization Project

From: Poppi
To: La Bella Verita
Sent: Autumn

Thought of the Day:
The only man who never makes a mistake is the man who
never does anything.
Theodore Roosevelt

From: Poppi
To: La Bella Verita
Sent: Autumn

Thought of the Day:
To create one's own world takes courage.
Georgia O'Keeffe

From: Poppi
To: La Bella Verita
Sent: Autumn

Thought of the Day:
What's important is that one strives to achieve a goal.
Ronald Reagan

From: Poppi
To: La Bella Verita
Sent: Autumn

Thought of the Day:
Trust in your own untried capacity.
Ella Wheeler Wilcox

From: Poppi
To: La Bella Verita
Sent: Autumn

Thought of the Day:
The hardest struggle of all is to be something different from
what the average man is.
Charles M. Schwab

From: Poppi
To: La Bella Verita
Sent: Spring

Thought of the Day:
Every man believes that he has a greater possibility.
Ralph Waldo Emerson

From: Poppi
To: La Bella Verita
Sent: Spring

Thought of the Day:
Create a legacy of celebration. Celebrate yourself in a way that
affirms your identity, your history, your presence, and the possibility you envision for your life.
Dr. Harvey L. Rich

From: Poppi
To: La Bella Verita
Sent: Autumn

Thought of the Day:
Life is measured in Moments, not in years.
Anonymous

From: Poppi
To: La Bella Verita
Sent: Autumn

Today is the first day of classes at the University. Here is a thought to carry you through.

Thought of the Day:
Dreams are what make Life bearable.
from the movie "Rudy"

From: Poppi
To: La Bella Verita
Sent: Autumn

Thought of the Day:
Fulfillment is the destination on every human being's journey of Life.

From: Poppi
To: La Bella Verita
Sent: Autumn

Thought of the Day:
Decide on a plan for Life's direction. But, when it comes to making decisions that affect your plan, make them on instinct rather than emotion.

From: Poppi
To: La Bella Verita
Sent: Autumn

Thought of the Day:
Always keep your Dreams out of reach but never out of sight.
Anonymous

From: Poppi
To: La Bella Verita
Sent: Winter

Thought of the Day:
There is satisfaction that is mighty sweet to take, when you reach a destination that you thought you'd never make.
Spirella

From: Poppi
To: La Bella Verita
Sent: Winter

Thought of the Day:
The first step on your Journey of Life begins with the mind and not the feet.

From: Poppi
To: La Bella Verita
Sent: Spring

Thought of the Day:
The most difficult period is the period of transition.

From: Poppi
To: La Bella Verita
Sent: Winter

Thought of the Day:
Life is an unbearable gift sometimes. Unbearably beautiful and unbearably painful, but always a gift.
Anonymous

From: Poppi
To: La Bella Verita
Sent: Winter

Thought of the Day:
You have to accept whatever comes and the only important thing is that you meet it with courage.
Eleanor Roosevelt

From: Poppi
To: La Bella Verita
Sent: Winter

Thought of the Day:
I learned to take one day at a time, and the future will take care of itself.
Rudy Guiliani

From: Poppi
To: La Bella Verita
Sent: Winter

Thought of the Day:
Things may happen for a reason, but sometimes things happen to give you a reason.
Anonymous

From: Poppi
To: La Bella Verita
Sent: Spring

Thought of the Day:
Avoiding danger is no safer in the long run than outright exposure. Life is either a daring adventure, or nothing.
Helen Keller

From: Poppi
To: La Bella Verita
Sent: Autumn

Thought of the Day:
Consult not your fears but your hopes and dreams. Think not about what you have tried and failed, but what is still possible for you to do. To Live is to Change.
Anonymous

From: Poppi
To: La Bella Verita
Sent: Spring

Thought of the Day:
Understand the past, anticipate the future, clarify the present.
Anonymous

From: Poppi
To: La Bella Verita
Sent: Autumn

Thought of the Day:
Your aspirations are your possibilities
Samuel Johnson

From: Poppi
To: La Bella Verita
Sent: Autumn

Thought of the Day:
You don't just go through life, but you grow through life.

From: Poppi
To: La Bella Verita
Sent: Winter

How are you doing on your studying?

Thought of the Day:
Every period of study is like a stepping stone up the mountain
of achievement. Even a setback elevates you up one more
step because it is experience learned for another time. As you
move from one stepping stone to the next, you may not feel
like progress is being made. But, when you reach a "Plateau of
Growth" and turn around, you realize how far you have come
on the journey.

From: Poppi
To: La Bella Verita
Sent: Winter

Thought of the Day:
The PAST - Provides a basis of knowledge
(What has been done)
The FUTURE - Holds a promise of a Dream
(What can be done)
The PRESENT - Has the potential for action
(What will be done)

From: Poppi
To: La Bella Verita
Sent: Winter

Thought of the Day:
Never, ever, look back. Something might be gaining.
Satchel Paige

From: Poppi
To: La Bella Verita
Sent: Autumn

Thought of the Day:
You don't have to be afraid of change. You don't have to worry
about what's being taken away. Just look to see what's been
added.
Jackie Greer

From: Poppi
To: La Bella Verita
Sent: Autumn

Thought of the Day:
It is never too late to become what you might have been.
George Eliot

From: Poppi
To: La Bella Verita
Sent: Autumn

Mom & I watched the final show of the American Idol's first
season last night. We followed the competition all summer. I
didn't realize it was such a big event on the college campuses.

Thought of the Day:
The show is a lesson in itself because it has the basic elements of enjoying life. Each contestant has an "ASPIRATION"
to achieve a dream; each contestant knows that it doesn't
happen overnight but is rather a "JOURNEY"; and each has to
have a "REALITY CHECK" along the way, which allows them to
reevaluate and adjust to continue toward achieving their goal.

From: Poppi
To: La Bella Verita
Sent: Autumn

Thought of the Day:
At age 67, Thomas Edison watched as a fire destroyed his life
long work and equipment. Instead of retiring he said "all our
mistakes are burned up, now we can start anew".
The fire burned his work, but not the fire within him to go on.

From: Poppi
To: La Bella Verita
Sent: Autumn

Thought of the Day:
Nothing in life just happens. You have to have the stamina to
meet the obstacles and overcome them.
Golda Meir

From: Poppi
To: La Bella Verita
Sent: Autumn

Thought of the Day:
If you want the rainbow, you got to put up with the rain.
Dolly Parton

From: Poppi
To: La Bella Verita
Sent: Winter

Thought of the Day:
The trouble is, if you don't risk anything, you risk even more.
Erica Jong

From: Poppi
To: La Bella Verita
Sent: Winter

Thought of the Day:
Strength comes from RISK...if you succeed, you will "Be in a stronger position than before". If you fail, there will be the feeling of failure, hurt, the healing process and eventually gaining strength that will bring you back to "Be in a stronger position than before".

From: Poppi
To: La Bella Verita
Sent: Winter

Thought of the Day:
When you are in a valley, keep the goal firmly in view and you will get the renewed energy to continue the climb.
Coach Bill Finney

From: Poppi
To: La Bella Verita
Sent: Winter

Thought of the Day:
Dream. Expect that everything will not go as planned, and believe that any adjustments will succeed.

From: Poppi
To: La Bella Verita
Sent: Spring

Thought of the Day:
No one has all the answers, but as long as you keep heading in
the right direction....the future will be bright.

From: Poppi
To: La Bella Verita
Sent: Autumn

Thought of the Day:
Everyone makes a wrong turn, but the importance is in understanding why it happened and getting back on the right course.

From: Poppi
To: La Bella Verita
Sent: Autumn

Thought of the Day:
I find the great thing in this world is not so much where we
stand, as in what direction we are moving: To reach the port of
heaven, we must sail sometimes with the wind and sometimes
against it, but we must sail, and not drift, nor lie at anchor.
Oliver Wendell Holmes, Jr.

From: Poppi
To: La Bella Verita
Sent: Autumn

Thought of the Day:
To fly, we must have resistance.
Maya Lin, Architect

From: Poppi
To: La Bella Verita
Sent: Winter

Thought of the Day:
You don't get older by the years, you get newer by the day.
Emily Dickenson

From: Poppi
To: La Bella Verita
Sent: Autumn

Thought of the Day:
I am a slow walker, but I never walk backwards.
Abraham Lincoln

From: Poppi
To: La Bella Verita
Sent: Spring

Thought of the Day:
Springtime signals change as a time to move on.

From: Poppi
To: La Bella Verita
Sent: Autumn

Thought of the Day:
We come to Beginnings....only at the End
William Bridges

The Day of Trepidation September 11, 2001

NASA held a memorial remembrance ceremony on the tenth anniversary of the attack on America. The auditorium was filled to capacity as speakers presented their tribute. Headquarters is 1 1/2 city blocks from the House of Representatives Ford Office Building, so members of Congress were in attendance. Senator Bob Nelson, a former astronaut, spoke from his heart, but what made these few minutes of remembrance etched into the memories of all in attendance, was the solumn words from Astronaut Frank Culbertson. He was the only American who was not on this planet at the time of the attacks. He was on a mission on board the International Space Station (ISS).

Every morning, at 10:00 AM EST, the ISS would engage in a daily briefing with Mission Control. NASA Headquarters has a live feed to the ISS and airs the daily briefing live throughout the facility as well as to the public. There is a large screen that addresses the corner of 4th & E Street SW, as passersby can watch the briefings live. The first words from Mission Control to Astronaut Culbertson on September 11, 2001 were "We are not having a good day down here on Earth", and than proceeded to explain the terrorist attacks. The astronaut grabbed his camera and began taking photographs as the space ship flew over the eastern United States. The ISS travels at 17,150 mph and it takes 92 minutes to circle the earth. The audience expressed empathy as the photographs were shown as Astronaut Culbertson spoke.

This chapter has e mails from others than "Poppi". The date on the e mails are the same as on the original.

From: Nanni
To: Poppi
Sent: Tuesday, September 11, 2001 10:36 AM

She is off campus at Ballston, at class.

From: Poppi
To: Nanni
Sent: Tuesday, September 11, 2001 10:41 AM

Ballston, that is 4 subway stops from the Pentagon. She can probably see the smoke. By the way, both WTC Towers collapsed.

From: Nanni
To: Poppi
Sent: Tuesday, September 11, 2001 10:43 AM

We may close here......I may go get girls.

From: Poppi
To: Nanni
Sent: Tuesday, September 11, 2001 10:48 AM

Why would you do that. Stay off the damn roads!

From: Nanni
To: Poppi
Sent: Tuesday, September 11, 2001 11:18 AM

She is back on campus. She said it is crazy there. Everyone is trying to leave town. Find out if I can get there or not.

From: Poppi
To: Nanni
Sent: Tuesday, September 11, 2001 11:26 AM

You can't get on the roads. They are all shut down.

From: Poppi
To: Nanni
Sent: Tuesday, September 11, 2001 1:37 PM

She just called me. She is fine. They have no school tomorrow.

From: Nanni
To: Poppi
Sent: Tuesday, September 11, 2001 2:14 PM

Your sister called her. Your mom also e mailed her. Your brother was in California in August and should be back in New York City now, but no answer on his machine. He lives in the East Village. A girl at the school, her parent's work at the WTC, all the classmates went to church and the priest started crying. I think I will go to the chapel.

From: Poppi
To: La Bella Verita
Sent: September 12, 2001

Yesterday was the day that changed the United States. It brought home how evil people can be. We, as a people, need to destroy this condition. But, we first need to sit back and think, and not lash out. The terrorists acted in the name of religion. I do not know of any religion that sanctions the killing of innocent children, or even their own people. This is what misinformation & propaganda can lead to. That coupled with a mob mentality is dangerous. The world needs to deal with this or things will escalate. Yesterday's actions were an Act of War.

Thought of the Day:
Religion is not to be the basis for conflict or hatred, but rather a direction in the way to live one's life. No religion is based in creating a "holy War", only people who stray from the religious roots need a reason to war.

From: Auntie P
To: "D"
Sent: Tuesday, September 11, 2001 10:26 PM

Hey D, tried calling to check you out...tough to get through
phone lines. Just got word from mom that you are OK. Glad to
hear it. The kids were a little worried to. Drop us an e mail if
you get a chance. Hope you guys get through this disaster OK.
Let me know if there is anything we can do. If you want to get
away from New York City, Sunday is my son's 2nd Birthday. I'm
having a little brunch for him at 11:00 AM. We would love to see
you. Let me know.

From: "D"
To: Auntie P
Sent: Tuesday, September 12, 2001

Hello Auntie P.
My name is "D". I am from Sydney, Australia and received this e
mail from you in error.
I noticed the intended recipient must be from New York City.
I would like to take this opportunity to say that everybody in
Australia is shocked by the incidents that occurred in New York
on Tuesday night (our time). We had live news broadcasts
throughout the night and many people stayed up throughout the
night watching in horror as the events unfolded. Everybody is re-
morseful and the events have felt so close to home even though
we are half the world away.
I would like to share my feelings and the general feeling of the
Australian public with you. Everybody is very sympathetic and
empathetic to the American people.
I offer my sincerest condolences to you and your compatriots
and hope that the American people can recover from this tragedy
to be stronger & better than the people who have inflicted such
an atrocity.
Kindest Regards

From: Poppi
To: La Bella Verita
Sent: September 13, 2011

Yesterday was clearly a day of coming together. Driving to work
I noticed a lot of flags hanging from front porches, cars had flags
on them, and people were wearing red, white and blue. We
clearly are a strong people and show concern.

Thought of the Day:
The only thing necessary for the triumph of evil is for good men
to do nothing.
Edmund Burke

From: Poppi
To: La Bella Verita
Sent: September 14, 2001

Today is the National Day of Remembrance for the victims of
last Tuesday. Mom is wearing her USA shirt that she wore at
the Olympics. There will be services and moments of silence all
over the world.

Thought of the Day:
Faith, Prayers and Hope

From: Poppi
To: La Bella Verita
Sent: September 17, 2001

The terrorists may have destroyed a few symbols of America,
they will never destroy the "Idea" known as America.

Thought of the Day:
We the people of the United States of America, in order to form
a more perfect union, establish justice, insure domestic tran-
quility, provide for the common defense, promote the general
welfare, and secure the blessings of liberty.
The US Constitution Preamble   31

From: Poppi
To: La Bella Verita
Sent: September 18, 2001

Thought of the Day:
All of the excuses are no longer viable...all that matters now are
God and family.
from Sunday's Church Sermon

From: Poppi
To: La Bella Verita
Sent: September 19, 2001

Thought of the Day:
Monday, the sports world got back to playing baseball. The local TV sports announcer showed video of the opening ceremo-
nies from each ballpark and commented on the Mets players
wearing fireman hats from different fire stations in New York
City. The announcer ended the telecast without giving out the
scores...that didn't seem as important as just getting on with a
normal ballgame.

From: Poppi
To: La Bella Verita
Sent: September 21, 2001

Did you watch the president's speech last night? He answered
a lot of questions in simple terms while laying out a plan to
achieve a goal. He also leveled with the American people about
the reality of the mission.

Thought of the Day:
Leaders make their decisions by analysis and not from emo-
tions. These decisions are based on character, which is based
in right-wrong value judgements. A leader is not concerned
about the popular thoughts of the day. He leads by example
and not by perception. A leader elevates the performance of
others. There are those that will always show jealousy, disre-
spect or condemnation of the leader's decision. The leader will
always demonstrate understanding and patience.

From: Poppi
To: La Bella Verita
Sent: September 25, 2001

Thought of the Day:
The phrase "Prepare for the Unexpected" needs to be expanded
to "Prepare for the Unexpected and the Unthinkable."

From: Poppi
To: La Bella Verita
Sent: September 27, 2001

Thought of the Day:
When it is dark enough, you can see the stars.
Charles A. Beard

From: Poppi
To: La Bella Verita
Sent: October 3, 2001

So there probably won't be a "Midnight Madness" this year.
Well, it probably is for the best. The ramifications of 9-11 will be
felt for a long time.

Thought of the Day:
Our real blessings often appear to us in the SHAPES of pains,
losses, and disappointments; but let us have patience, and we
soon shall see them in their proper FIGURES.
Joseph Addison

From: Poppi
To: La Bella Verita
Sent: October 4, 2001

Thought of the Day:
The greater the obstacle, the more glory in overcoming it.
Moliere

From: Poppi
To: La Bella Verita
Sent: October 17, 2001

Did you ladies discuss the Anthrax situation? You know the
local Post Office was closed last Saturday because there was
a letter addressed to the White House with a return address
from London, England. It didn't have any postage and there
was a substance on it. The PO was shut down and roped off.
All of these people from Fort Detrick were there in Hazmet
suits. What they found out was that the letter came from a little
girl who is in the area with her family. They are from London,
England. The little girl and her cousin wanted to help the other
little boys and girls who lost their parents in the attack on 9-11.
So, they sent a dollar bill to the White House to help. Unfortu-
nately, they spilled soda on the envelope and didn't know about
postage.

Thought of the Day:
Let us not look back in anger, or forward in fear, but around in
awareness.
James Thurber

From: Poppi
To: La Bella Verita
Sent: November 28, 2001

Remember Grand pop got you ladies a subscription to the
Readers Digest as a gift one year. Well, it is still coming to the
house. The latest issue is dedicated to September 11, 2001.
There is an interview with Muhammad Ali. He was interviewed
on 9-11, just a coincidence. His interview is filled with emotion.
He is a Muslim and an American.

Thought of the Day:
Rivers, ponds, lakes, and streams all have different names, but
all contain water. Religions have different names but all contain
TRUTH.
Muhammad Ali

From: Poppi
To: La Bella Verita
Sent: December 3, 2001

The Christmas lights are up and the house looks festive. Mom and I took a walk through the neighborhood last night to see the different houses with lights on them. There seems to be more than other years. The theme this year is white lights, but some of the houses have mixed in lighted American flags. There are flags made from strings of red, white & blue Christmas lights. There is a more Patriotic feel this season. A new awareness to celebrate "The Birth" on December 25th.

Thought of the Day:
.....This nation, under God, shall have a new birth of Freedom- and that the government of the people, by the people, for the people, shall not perish from the earth.
President Abraham Lincoln
Gettysburg Address

From: Poppi
To: La Bella Verita
Sent: December 7, 2001

Today is the 60th anniversary of the Pearl Harbor attack. I am sure the newspapers will have numerous editorials about Pearl Harbor and the tie to September 11, 2001. Take a break and read a few. The articles could be enlightening.

Thought of the Day:
We can not change yesterday. We can only make the most of today, and look upon Hope toward tomorrow.
Anonymous

From: Poppi
To: La Bella Verita
Sent: December 19, 2001

I thought the following is fitting for the last Thought of the Day
of the semester. This is some of the Principal's message from
the monthly high school newsletter to parents.

Thought of the Day:

As we prepare for the upcoming holiday season it is not un-
common to discover a shift in our feelings toward Life. The
busy work routine that dominates our daily existence gives way
to warm feelings of caring and giving. We renew the desire to
change our life to include more happiness, more time for family,
and more time for ourselves.

The tragic events of 9-11 have challenged me to spend time
thinking about my own state of happiness.....Barbara DeAnge-
lis in her book "Real Moments" makes a profound statement,
"Happiness is not a state of being - it is a series of real moments."

It is my hope your holiday season is filled with much happiness.
I encourage you to search out your real moments. Don't make
this New Year's resolution to be more difficult than it needs to
be. Savior the moment. Let yourself find the happiness that ex-
ists within and around you.

Hal Mosser

From: Poppi
To: La Bella Verita
Sent: January 24, 2002

We just received the Marymount President's report: "A Season
of Continuity and Change"

Thought of the Day:

If the changes we are facing involve heightened awareness of
evil....the continuity we are experiencing involves Values that
are central to our national character.

Dr. James E. Bundschuh

From: Poppi
To: La Bella Verita
Sent: January 25, 2002

There is so much happening at the courthouse near Marymount. The American that was fighting with the terrorists is
there on trial.

Thought of the Day:
A person who doubts himself, is like a man who would enlist in
the ranks of his enemies and bear arms against himself.
Alexandre Dumas

From: Poppi
To: La Bella Verita
Sent: January 30, 2002

Did anyone watch the President's State of the Union? The
theme was preserving freedom, the American way of life and
security. He mentioned that these are the Affirmations that
people throughout the world hope for.

Thought of the Day:
People who acquire the Affirmations of America, do not become
Americanized, but do become humanized.

From: Poppi
To: La Bella Verita
Sent: February 2, 2002

Thought of the Day:
If there is right in the soul, there will be beauty in the person.
If there is beauty in the person, there will be harmony in the
home. If there is harmony in the home, there will be order in the
nation. If there is order in the nation, there will be peace in the
world.
Chinese Proverb

The Sustenance of Life

Faith, Family and Values

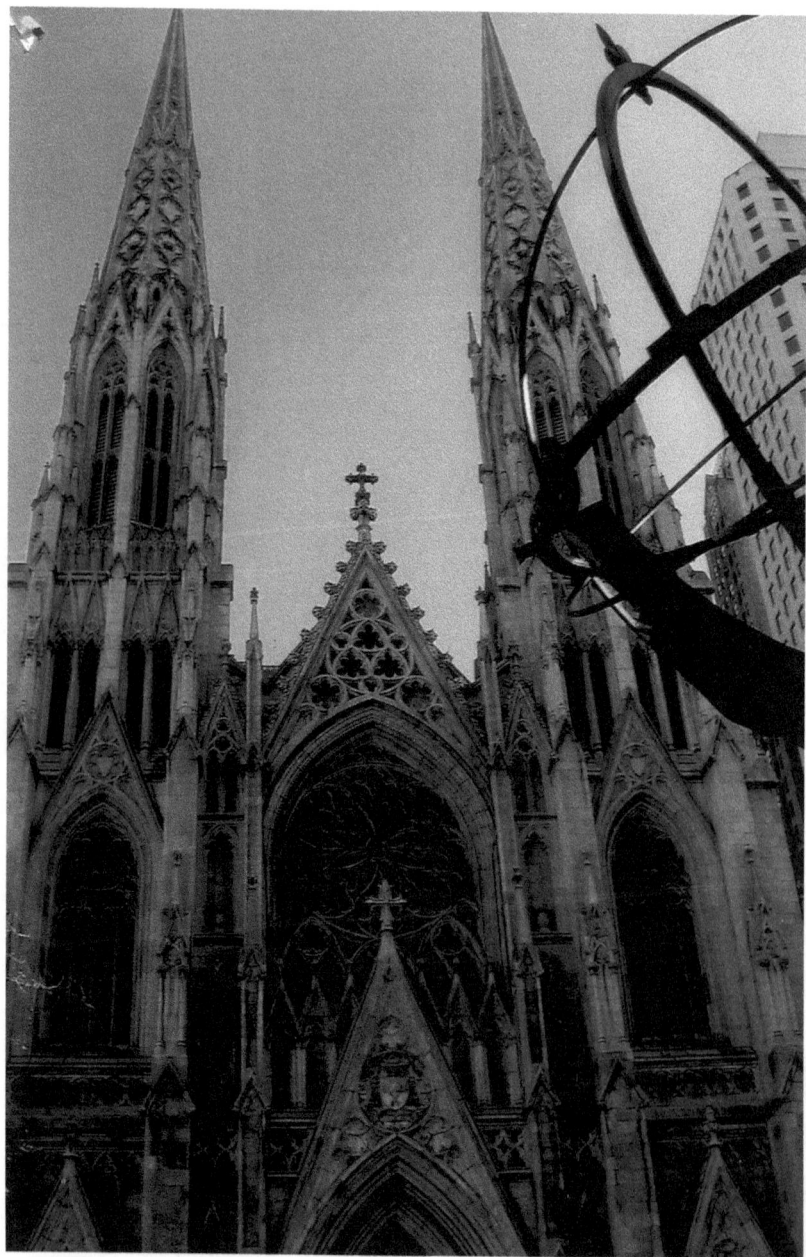

Faith

Originally, I listed Faith as the last category in the Sustenance of Life. Later I changed the order and made Faith the first and main category. It is the hardest to possess but yet it is the most important. Faith is the big jump to first in Believing, than integrating the belief system in daily conduct and events.

Ash Wednesday is a religious day in the Christian faith where ashes are placed on a person's head in remembrance that we will die and our body will deteriorate and return to the earth (ashes & dust). One Ash Wednesday, I was on the Science Mission Directorate floor and a planetary scientist said "You know we all come from Stardust". The scientist proceeded to write a name on a piece of paper and told me that I needed to read this scientist's work. It was Jesuit Brother Guy Consolmagno, from the Vatican Observatory. He is the first clergyman to receive planetary science's most prestigious award, the Carl Sagan Medal.

Human Beings are flawed. We make major errors that affect our daily lives. We have an inner drive to make our lives better. The easier it is to live in this world, the easier it is to loose Faith. Every day becomes convenient and we become arrogant in believing that our plan is the only plan. We all have an ego which gives us self-confidence to achieve. When self-confidence turns into selfishness, than arrogance takes over. Arrogance pulls us away from the heart of Faith which Paul so elegantly writes to the Ephesians [4:1-4]:
I....urge you to live in a manner worthy of the call you have received, with all humility and gentleness, with patience, bearing with one another through love, striving to preserve the unity of the spirit through the bond of peace; one body and one spirit, as you were also called to the one hope of your call......Grace was given to each of us.

From: Poppi
To: La Bella Verita
Sent: Winter

Thought of the Day:
Faith is the Mortar that holds our Moral Foundation together.

From: Poppi
To: La Bella Verita
Sent: Autumn

Halloween is the Season's Party Scene.
The day after is All Soul's Day. It is a day to remember people who have passed on. Take a little time and remember the goodness that those people brought.

Thought of the Day:
Everyone has both good and bad qualities. Only remember the goodness in the people that have passed on. We walk this earth for a short period of time but by passing down our goodness, makes us immortal.

From: Poppi
To: La Bella Verita
Sent: Winter

Thought of the Day:
Do not wish to be anything but what you are, and try to be that perfectly.
St. Francis De Sales

From: Poppi
To: La Bella Verita
Sent: Winter

Thought of the Day:
The desire accomplished is sweet to the soul.
King Solomon from Proverbs 13:19

From: Poppi
To: La Bella Verita
Sent: Winter

Thought of the Day:
At God's footstool to confess
A poor soul knelt and bowed his head
"I failed" he cried. The Master said
"Thou didst thy best, that is success."
Anonymous

From: Poppi
To: La Bella Verita
Sent: Spring

Thought of the Day:
During Easter Mass, the priest asked 6 questions in renewing
our purpose in Life:
3 questions on Moral Values
3 questions on the Mystery of Faith
They are serious questions to ponder on the direction of life to
lead. The priest's sermon was based on "Never giving up on
your journey." Therefore, think about the questions, and use the
affirmation as the basis on your journey in life.

From: Poppi
To: La Bella Verita
Sent: Spring

We just received the latest Zornicka (Slovak Magazine) from
Grand mom. It has a nice article about Lent and the Easter
season.

Thought of the Day:
3 Words
REMEMBER - Who and What really matters
REPENT - Recognize areas of imperfection which have devel-
oped and make a conscious choice to turn away from them.
RECOMMIT - to be a better Christian
Father Philip A. Altavilla

From: Poppi
To: La Bella Verita
Sent: Winter

> Mom and I were talking to a few of the parents after last night's game. They told us how after the Catholic University game the team got together in prayer. They said the team really gave comfort to Katie after losing her Grandmother.

Thought of the Day:
There are many questions during an individual's "Period of Transition.", But there is only 1 true universal answer.......Prayer

From: Poppi
To: La Bella Verita
Sent: Autumn

> Mom was reading the Bible last night before bed. She said that all of her hospital management meetings start with a quote from the Bible. She needs to read 1 before today's meeting.

Thought of the Day:
A cord of 3 is seldom broken.
Ecclesiastes 4:12

From: Poppi
To: La Bella Verita
Sent: Spring

> Tori's communion was nice. Afterward Great-Grand mom told us she is cancer free. She stopped treatments because they made her sick. The cancer is not in remission, it is gone.

Thought of the Day:
Sometime you just need to "Believe in the Mystery", and don't bother with the analysis of the phenomenon.

From: Poppi
To: La Bella Verita
Sent: Winter

There isn't much you could have done with only 7 players against the 25th ranked team. With all the 6 foot post players and the leading scorer (not to mention All American) out was a little too much to overcome. Your team didn't give up. Time to regroup and move forward.

Thought of the Day:
PERSISTENCE
I am only 1 but I am 1. I can't do everything, but I can do something. That what I can do, I will do. So if I can run, I will run. If I can walk, I will walk. If I can crawl, I will crawl. But with God's help, I will always move forward.
Norman Vincent Peale

From: Poppi
To: La Bella Verita
Sent: Autumn

We had a ton of little kids last night for Halloween. It was a nice sight with the fear of something happening because of 9-11. At least that is the way the media portrayed the situation. How was Halloween at college?
Once again, now today is All Soul's Day. This day is a little more somber than the others because of the loss of life on 9-11 and the War on Terrorism. I am sure the church sermons will reflect on how uncertain life is.

Thought of the Day:
A Mortal thought of someone special that has passed on bridges the "Immortality" Divide.

From: Poppi
To: La Bella Verita
Sent: Spring

Mom forwarded me the Hospital's Monday Meditation. It's a good one.

Thought of the Day:
"We will sit as a refiner and purifier of silver."
There was a group of women in a Bible study on the book of Malachi. As they were studying chapter 3, they came across this verse.

This verse puzzled the women and they wondered what this statement meant about the character and nature of God. One of the women offered to find out about the process of refining silver and get back to the group at their next Bible study session.

That week this woman called a silversmith and made an appointment to watch him at work. As she watched the silversmith, he held a piece of silver over the fire and let it heat up. He explained that in refining silver, one needs to hold the silver in the middle of the fire where the flames were hottest so as to burn away all the impurities.

She asked the silversmith if it is true that he had to sit there in front of the fire the whole time the silver was being refined. The man answered that yes, he not only had to sit there holding the silver, but he had to keep his eyes on the silver the entire time it was in the fire. For if the silver is left even a moment too long in the flames, it would be destroyed.

The woman was silent for a moment. Then she asked the silversmith, how do you know when the silver is fully refined? He smiled at her and answered, "Oh, that's the easy part. It is when I see my image reflected in it."

If today you are feeling the heat of the fire, remember that God has His eye on you and will keep His hand on you and watch over you until He sees His image in you.
William C. Robertson
President & CEO
Adventist Healthcare Inc.

From: Poppi
To: La Bella Verita
Sent: Spring

Yesterday was the first day of Holy Week. Mom and I went to
Mass at St. John's in downtown Frederick, Maryland. The hom-
ily was about the "Beatitudes". A set of core teachings of Christ.
The sermon was on how the Beatitudes relate to today. I asked
the priest for a copy of his sermon since it was so thoughtful
and a good basis for having Humility. There are eight and a
short story, I will send each as a separate Thought of the Day.

Thought of the Day:
If you are struggling to pay the bills, but insist on making time
to be with your children whenever they need you, Blessed are
you - you may never own the big vacation home, but heaven
will be yours..

From: Poppi
To: La Bella Verita
Sent: Spring

Thought of the Day:
If you are overwhelmed by the care of a dying spouse, a sick
child, or an elderly parent, but you are determined to make a
loving home for them, Blessed are you - one day your sorrow
will be transformed into joy.

From: Poppi
To: La Bella Verita
Sent: Spring

Thought of the Day:
If you willingly give time to cook at a soup kitchen, dust the
church, or help in a classroom; if you befriend the uncool, the
unpopular, the perpetually lost, Blessed are you - count God
among your friends and biggest boosters.

From: Poppi
To: La Bella Verita
Sent: Spring

Thought of the Day:

If you refuse to take shortcuts when it comes to doing what is right, if you refuse to compromise your integrity and ethics, if you refuse to take refuge in the rationalization that "everybody else is doing it", Blessed are you - you will triumph.

From: Poppi
To: La Bella Verita
Sent: Spring

Thought of the Day:

If you try to understand things from the perspective of the other person and always manage to find a way to make things work for the good; if you are feeling discouraged and frustrated because you are always bending over backwards, always forgiving the undeserving, Blessed are you - God will welcome, and forgive and love you.

From: Poppi
To: La Bella Verita
Sent: Spring

Thought of the Day:

If you struggle to discover what God asks of you in all things; if you seek God's presence in every facet of your life and every decision you make; if your constant prayer to God is not "Give me" but "Help me", Blessed are you - God will always be there for you.

From: Poppi
To: La Bella Verita
Sent: Spring

Thought of the Day:

I went for a walk and stayed out till sundown. For going out, I found what was really going on.

John Muir

From: Poppi
To: La Bella Verita
Sent: Spring

Thought of the Day:
If you readily spend time listening and consoling anyone who looks to you for compassion; if you manage to heal wounds and build bridges; if others see in you graciousness, joy, and serenity; if you can see good in everyone and seek the good for everyone, Blessed are you - you are nothing less than God's own.

From: Poppi
To: La Bella Verita
Sent: Spring

Thought of the Day:
If you are rejected or demeaned because of the color of your skin or the sound of your name; if your faith automatically puts you at odds with some people; if you refuse to go along with the crowd because of what you know in your heart, Blessed are you - One day you will live with God.

From: Poppi
To: La Bella Verita
Sent: Spring

Thought of the Day:
You may have heard of the man who stayed behind with a person in a wheel chair on 9-11. His 70 year old sister grieved his loss deeply, and went to Afghanistan as part of her grieving. She shared her grief with Afghans who were suffering as a result of the same evil forces. Now, she has returned to the USA and is raising money to assist grieving Afghans. At 70 she is taking seriously the words of Jesus, "Blessed are they who mourn, for they will be comforted."

From: Poppi
To: La Bella Verita
Sent: Winter

A lot of snow, over 3 feet in some areas.

Thought of the Day:
Snow days can be boring or they can be exciting. Boring if you have the attitude that it limits you (mobility). Exciting if you have the attitude that it is God sent to free up time to do something more important.

From: Poppi
To: La Bella Verita
Sent: Autumn

It is good that the team has a daily "Spiritual" gathering at the end of every practice. It doesn't matter what the sport is; Basketball, Lacrosse, etc., It is always good to stop and give thanks for the opportunity to "Grow". "Grow" in both athletics and as a person.

Thought of the Day:
There are three parts of our existence: the mind, the body and the soul. Time set aside for daily spiritual contemplation provides confidence for the mind, energy for the body and peace for the soul.

From: Poppi
To: La Bella Verita
Sent: Autumn

Thought of the Day:
If you hold up your head with a smile on your face and are truly thankful, you are blessed because the majority of us can, but most do not.
Anonymous

Family

Families establish an intergenerational bond. The family allows a person growing up that he/she belongs to something bigger than themselves. Families have a core identity. Each generation preserves this identity while stimulating progress. Families have a story to tell. The story has positive family moments and difficult ones that show the ability to bounce back and move on. Stories, customs and traditions become part of the family.

It is no secret that human enterprises, from companies to countries, have learned from the basic family unit. It has been overheard many times, "Where I work is like a family". That is, the business goes out of it's way to capture a core identity, just like the true intergenerational family.

From: Poppi
To: La Bella Verita
Sent: Autumn

Good Morning,
Please e mail your mother today because it is our 20th Wedding
Anniversary. I am probably going to take her some place special
in the spring. We just can't get away right now.

Thought of the Day:
Love is Timeless

From: Poppi
To: La Bella Verita
Sent: Autumn

Grand mom said she sent you an e-mail. Who would have
thought a few years ago that a 72 year old would be sending e-
mails to a college student.

Thought of the Day:
You know you have grown when you come home and the feeling
isn't exactly what it used to be.

From: Poppi
To: La Bella Verita
Sent: Autumn

Grand mom read me the e-mail that you sent her. She is so
proud, she printed it out and is showing everyone.

Thought of the Day:
Mothers and Grandmothers are the "Coaches" in the game of
Life.

From: Poppi
To: La Bella Verita
Sent: Autumn

Now that Grand mom sent you an e-mail from her work computer, Grand pop now said he is going to get a computer soon. He
said he needs to e-mail you on how to get rid of a "Pain in the
A#$" boy. Look out, he may be e-mailing you all day long.

Thought of the Day:
Fathers and Grandfathers are the "Teachers of Values".

From: Poppi
To: La Bella Verita
Sent: Autumn

So you have Trick or Treaters at the Dorm. That is so cool. Little
kids get enjoyment out of the simplest things. How about that
little boy in the Rainforest Cafe who thought the thunderstorm
was real and jumped into his Daddy's lap.

Thought of the Day:
We are put on this earth to teach the children but sometimes the
children teach us.

From: Poppi
To: La Bella Verita
Sent: Autumn

It was nice to have the family together for Thanksgiving. It was
good food and fun conversation about growing up. Now you are
back at school and eating the cafeteria food....YUMMM.

Thought of the Day:
One Moment in childhood, a door opens and let's the Future in.

From: Poppi
To: La Bella Verita
Sent: Winter

Mom and I went and got a Christmas Tree yesterday. Our family tradition is always cut down a tree, the first weekend in December. It has been 20 years now that we have been doing the same thing: Go to the tree farm, walk around (or when you girls were little, run around), find the perfect tree, cut it down, bring it home, put it up and watch it fall over.

Well, this year, I think we did get the perfect tree, although it is kind of chubby, it is straight and the perfect height.

Thought of the Day:
The timeless repetition of Family Tradition, whether it be in physical or spiritual presence, brings everyone together.

From: Poppi
To: La Bella Verita
Sent: Winter

Grand mom and Grand pop will be down on Christmas. It doesn't matter where we take them, they will always act like Grand mom and Grand pop (you know what I mean)

Thought of the Day:
There will be a time when teenagers view their Grandparents as providing "Embarrassed Excitement", but Grandparents will always view Grandchildren as providing "Excited Embellishment".

From: Poppi
To: La Bella Verita
Sent: Winter

Thought of the Day:
You have now graduated to that elusive age group that can use the term: "Going home for the Holidays".

From: Poppi
To: La Bella Verita
Sent: Winter

Thought of the Day:
Happy Birthday,
Birthdays are not only a gauge on physical age but also a barometer on how far your "Frame of Reference" expanded in a year.

From: Poppi
To: La Bella Verita
Sent: Winter

You said it was nice to be home and rest, even though it was just for recovery from appendix surgery. I think the whole family felt relieved and calm.

Thought of the Day:
Like a quilt, family is at peace, when the pieces are one.
Hatfield

From: Poppi
To: La Bella Verita
Sent: Winter

Mom made Christmas cookies last night. She was happy because she got to use her cookie cutters from when she was a small child........AHHH, the smell of Christmas baking. Soon enough, you will smell it too.

Thought of the Day:
A memento from a time past always brings out good memories.

From: Poppi
To: La Bella Verita
Sent: Winter

Thought of the Day:
Every birthday is a day to wonder whether you have changed or grown over the past year. Change can be either good or bad, where Growing is always in a positive direction.

From: Poppi
To: La Bella Verita
Sent: Autumn

Mom will be down to pick you up after basketball practice. You may have to go food shopping with her on the way back....pick out something tasty for the big meal.

Thought of the Day:
Thanksgiving has become the "Family Day" of America. It is the one day to stop and appreciate the relationships of life; Family, Friends, Community and of course You for being You.

From: Poppi
To: La Bella Verita
Sent: Winter

We went and got the Christmas tree on Saturday. It was raining but that did not stop the family tradition of prancing thru the woods. It was just as much fun this year as before, of course, it was more fun when you girls were little and always picking out a tree that doesn't stand up straight; and when I put it up and it fell down, you always blamed it on me.

Thought of the Day:
Enjoyment of a family tradition brings sunshine on a rainy day.

From: Poppi
To: La Bella Verita
Sent: Winter

Everyone is coming to the Holiday Tournament. Grand mom and
Grand pop are staying with us and will be coming to the first
game with us. Aunt P. and her crew will be going to the game
first and then to the hotel. Maybe Uncle D. can come down from
New York City.

Thought of the Day:
Sometimes the best Christmas present is just "Being Present".

From: Poppi
To: La Bella Verita
Sent: Winter

Thought of the Day:
Instead of making a Birthday wish, share a Birthday dream. A
wish is nothing but whimsical desire. A Dream can be visual-
ized, and a plan can be put in place to make your "Birthday
Dream" a reality.

From: Poppi
To: La Bella Verita
Sent: Spring

Thought of the Day:
Easter is a time for renewing the family.

From: Poppi
To: La Bella Verita
Sent: Autumn

Thought of the Day:
Parents are not here to dampen your fun, but here to limit the
misery.
Dr. Laura

From: Poppi
To: La Bella Verita
Sent: Autumn

Well, Grand pop called the house three times last night to give me directions to the Penn State football game. I guess he is excited to go.

Thought of the Day:
The older you get, the more you appreciate little things, like going to a football game with your son.

From: Poppi
To: La Bella Verita
Sent: Winter

I hope the information on the family tree is helpful. You are only a third generation American. There is still one of the original immigrants (Great-Grand mom) that is still alive and kicking.

Thought of the Day:
One can see the "Dream of America" in an immigrant's set of eyes.

From: Poppi
To: La Bella Verita
Sent: Winter

Everyone had a fun time at Great-Grand mom's birthday party. There were relatives there that we haven't seen in a decade or longer. It was nice that so many people came. Great-Grand mom looks good.

Thought of the Day:
The measure of a person's life is reflected in the family.

From: Poppi
To: La Bella Verita
Sent: Spring

Mom had a really nice Mother's Day with all of us. I hope you did too.

Thought of the Day:
Mom's have all of the answers. You just don't realize it until you are well into your 30's.

From: Poppi
To: La Bella Verita
Sent: Autumn

Thought of the Day:
You learn valuable lessons about life when you are with the extended family (aunts, uncles, cousins, nieces, and nephews), because you are placed in a position of family observer.

From: Poppi
To: La Bella Verita
Sent: Autumn

Thanksgiving break........AHHH, the smell of turkey, family laughter (or loudness), getting caught up on the happenings of the semester, getting prepared for finals (or anxiety), and of course the loads and loads of college laundry.
See you in a day.

Thought of the Day:
Taking time to "Give Thanks" is an every Thursday thing.

Values

Thinking about the Values and Principles that you are going to live by is the basis of decision making that will eventually bring your dream to fruition or destroy it. The Values and Principles are passed down from your family and are interwoven with your faith. These are the Right-Wrong judgements that are made interacting with others. Decisions made in honesty and truth will always be respected by others.

From: Poppi
To: La Bella Verita
Sent: Autumn

Thought of the Day:
Responsibility and friendship are on two different levels. A leader has the ability to make a responsible decision that can develop a friendship. If the friend is true, the decision will be respected. In the end, both participants must be content with their own decision.

From: Poppi
To: La Bella Verita
Sent: Autumn

Thought of the Day:
Perseverance builds both physical and mental confidence.

From: Poppi
To: La Bella Verita
Sent: Autumn

Thought of the Day:
To build character, one must start from the Podium of Responsibility.

From: Poppi
To: La Bella Verita
Sent: Autumn

Thought of the Day:
Life is short.......but there is always time to support a friend.

From: Poppi
To: La Bella Verita
Sent: Winter

Thought of the Day:
It is one of the most beautiful compensations of this life that no man can sincerely try to help another without helping himself.
Emerson

From: Poppi
To: La Bella Verita
Sent: Winter

Thought of the Day:
I was riding the subway in DC and overheard 2 people talking. One said "What a miserable day". The other person responded with "It is a wonderful day, what does the weather have to do with it?" Attitude makes a difference in one's view of the world.

From: Poppi
To: La Bella Verita
Sent: Spring

Thought of the Day:
Nothing in the world can take the place of Persistence. Talent will not; nothing is more common than unsuccessful men with talent. Genius will not; unrewarded genius is almost a proverb. Education will not; the world is full of educated derelicts. Persistence and determination are omnipotent.
Calvin Coolidge

From: Poppi
To: La Bella Verita
Sent: Autumn

Thought of the Day:
Tolerance provides an opportunity for understanding.

65

From: Poppi
To: La Bella Verita
Sent: Autumn

Parent's weekend was nice. The Awards ceremony and Inauguration of the New University President were both excellent. He
seems like he is going to be good for the University. The Mass
was enlightening with the Bishop and all....and the Jazz Brunch
was fun.

Thought of the Day:
The Ideals which have always shown before me and filled me
with the joy of living are Goodness, Beauty and Truth.
Albert Einstein

From: Poppi
To: La Bella Verita
Sent: Winter

Thought of the Day:
Good habits are just as hard to break as bad ones.
Colleen Marish Rae

From: Poppi
To: La Bella Verita
Sent: Autumn

Thought of the Day:
Continuity gives us roots; Change gives us branches: allowing
us to stretch and grow to reach new heights.
Pauline R. Kezer

From: Poppi
To: La Bella Verita
Sent: Autumn

Thought of the Day:
The price of greatness is responsibility.
Winston Churchill

From: Poppi
To: La Bella Verita
Sent: Autumn

Thought of the Day:
S-Smile
M-Meet and Learn about people
I-Initiate; don't complain, but do something about it
L-Love; not Attraction but a decision to hold someone or something in great honor
E-Enjoy what you have
Gary Williams, President, Coakley-Williams Hotel Management Inc.

From: Poppi
To: La Bella Verita
Sent: Autumn

I understand that instead of going to the library, you went to a "Questionable" place.

Thought of the Day:
NEVER....EVER....Sell your soul, because if you do.....you will NEVER....EVER get it back.
Harriet Simmel (Grand mom Sam)

From: Poppi
To: La Bella Verita
Sent: Winter

Thought of the Day:
"Hard Work" in a structured manner, taking "Criticism" while developing successful relationships and "Cooperation" are key elements of "Self-Confidence".

From: Poppi
To: La Bella Verita
Sent: Winter

Thought of the Day:
The attitude that you portray is dependent upon 2 values: the value of "Inner Belief"; believing without pause that you are worthy, and the value of "Self-Confidence"; confident that whatever happens will eventually end in a positive venture.

From: Poppi
To: La Bella Verita
Sent: Spring

Tournament time is right around the corner for one of you. Lacrosse season is starting for the other. Both are opportunities for showing leadership abilities.

Thought of the Day:
Develop and Communicate Strong Beliefs; Reflect, then Decide; Organize around a Purpose; Prepare Relentlessly.
Rudolph W. Giuliani, Titles from his book Leadership.

From: Poppi
To: La Bella Verita
Sent: Winter

Thought of the Day:
Part of Leadership is harnessing your passions in a way that serves your goals. But another part of Leadership is retaining your Humanity. The challenge is to put them to work in ways that would make a stronger, better leader.
Rudolph W. Giuliani

From: Poppi
To: La Bella Verita
Sent: Autumn

Looks like a hurricane is heading our way.

Thought of the Day:

Maybe the reason there is a "Calm before the Storm" is to allow pause and be reminded that the awesome power of nature sets the rules.

From: Poppi
To: La Bella Verita
Sent: Autumn

Thought of the Day:

If you do a good job for others, you heal yourself at the same time, because a dose of joy is a spiritual cure.
Dietrich Bonhoeffer

From: Poppi
To: La Bella Verita
Sent: Spring

Thought of the Day:

The Greatness of work is in the Man.
Pope John Paul I I

From: Poppi
To: La Bella Verita
Sent: Spring

Thought of the Day:

Responsibility is the main ingredient of a healthy future.

From: Poppi
To: La Bella Verita
Sent: Autumn

Thought of the Day:

A daughter went to her mother and told her how things were so
hard for her. She did not know how she was going to make it
and wanted to give up. She was tired of fighting and struggling.
It seemed as one problem was solved a new one arose.

Her mother took her to the kitchen. She filled three pots with
water. In the first, she placed carrots, in the second she placed
eggs and the last she placed ground coffee beans. She let
them all sit and boil. After twenty minutes she took all the pots
off the stove and emptied them into bowls.

Turning to her daughter, she asked, What do you see?". The
daughter answered carrots, eggs and coffee. "What's the point,
mother?"

Her mother explained that each of these objects had faced
the same adversity...boiling water...but each reacted differently.
The carrot went in strong, hard and unrelenting. However after
being subjected to the boiling water, it softened and became
weak. The egg had been fragile. It's thin outer shell had protected its liquid interior. But, after sitting through the boiling
water, it's inside became hardened. The ground beans were
unique, however. After they were in the boiling water they had
changed the water.

"Which are you?", She asked her daughter. "Which one can
you become? Are you like a carrot that seems strong, but with
pain and adversity, do you wilt, become soft and lose strength?
Are you an egg that starts out with a malleable heart and a
fluid spirit. But when some trial comes along, do you become
hardened and stiff? Your outside shell looks the same, but
inside you are bitter with a hardened heart? Or are you like the
coffee bean? The bean actually changes the hot water, the very
circumstance that brings the pain. When the water gets hot, it
releases the fragrance and flavor. If you are like the bean, when
things are at their worst, you get better and change the situation
around you.

Submitted by Kate from an internet site.

The Foundation of Fulfillment

Learn, Compete and Create

Learn

Once a week at NASA, the Science Mission Directorate would provide a "Lunch and Learn" presentation on a scientific topic. I had the science coordinator add my name to receive weekly invitations. I attended a majority of these presentations. Scientists in the fields of Astrophysics, Astrobiology, Heliophysics, Planetary Science and Human Exploration gave presentations. The scientists, realizing that the audience was not all scientists, kept the presentation at a high level. The presentations were fascinating and fluid. There was never a definitive "The Science is settled". Rather, somewhere in every presentation, the phrase, "We just don't know", or "This is the best we know right now", was mentioned. There is always more to discover or uncover.

Education is a daily experience. Formal education gives the basis for interaction. The pursuit of your happiness will allow you to direct your time in learning what is needed to work within the area of your livelihood plan. For example. If you want to pursue Architecture, you need to specifically be taught in the profession, if you want to become an electrician, you will need to be trained and taught electricity and it's application. Successful people add another part of the education process. They are self-taught on aspects that others pursuing the same livelihood do not think are important or below the profession. An aspiring restaurant owner needs to learn the food and beverage business but should also be taught (even if it means being self-taught) in being a waiter or bartender. An aspiring home builder will need to be educated in real estate investment but also will need to know how to dig a foundation. The more you read about successful people your eyes will become open to the jobs that they wanted to learn, even though they may have never had to perform them. Their Frame of Reference gets expanded and a deeper understanding of their dream pursuit is appreciated. The passion to learn is in every one of us.

From: Poppi
To: La Bella Verita
Sent: Autumn

Thought of the Day:
If better is possible, good is not enough.

From: Poppi
To: La Bella Verita
Sent: Autumn

Thought of the Day:
When your desk gets cluttered, stop whatever task you are working on and clean it up. This will force you to reorganize your thoughts, which in turn will re-energize you to attack the task at hand.

From: Poppi
To: La Bella Verita
Sent: Autumn

Thought of the Day:
If you need people to help you work on a good cause, always ask the people that are busy and seem never to have any time. The people that have nothing to do will always find excuses not to participate. Busy people always find the time.

From: Poppi
To: La Bella Verita
Sent: Autumn

Thought of the Day:
A "Natural Environment" is when people feel comfortable to interact without consequence on a specific topic. To get the best results, make the class a "Natural Environment" by making the audience part of the presentation.

From: Poppi
To: La Bella Verita
Sent: Autumn

Thought of the Day:
Always put a monetary value on your goal. This will push you toward achievement, because now the goal becomes tangible instead of abstract.

From: Poppi
To: La Bella Verita
Sent: Autumn

Thought of the Day:
A decision made in haste usually means a redo. Gather the information, think, and make the decision based on intelligence.

From: Poppi
To: La Bella Verita
Sent: Winter

Thought of the Day:
Study review is like creating a window in a wall. Every time you review a topic, you remove a block in the wall. Eventually, you will see the brightness of day.

From: Poppi
To: La Bella Verita
Sent: Winter

Thought of the Day:
What makes a student succeed at the next level not only depends on how they prepared for their finals, but also their attitude when the exam is finished. Some study to remember, while some study to forget.

From: Poppi
To: La Bella Verita
Sent: Winter

Thought of the Day:
The people who succeed are the ones that put the extra effort and time into a subject, and therefore will perform better than the status quo.

From: Poppi
To: La Bella Verita
Sent: Winter

Thought of the Day:
Use the experience of your first semester in college to build on. Set those priorities high and work hard to achieve.

From: Poppi
To: La Bella Verita
Sent: Winter

Thought of the Day:
No one can make you feel inferior without your consent.
Eleanor Roosevelt

From: Poppi
To: La Bella Verita
Sent: Spring

Thought of the Day:
If you do not have the time to do it right, when will you find the time to do it over?
John Wooden

From: Poppi
To: La Bella Verita
Sent: Spring

Thought of the Day:
Goals achieved with little effort are seldom worthwhile.

From: Poppi
To: La Bella Verita
Sent: Spring

Thought of the Day:
The college learning experience doesn't end in the lab. Make
the world your classroom.

From: Poppi
To: La Bella Verita
Sent: Spring

Thought of the Day:
The college experience is one of many keys that open the door
of opportunity. Do not misplace the keys.

From: Poppi
To: La Bella Verita
Sent: Spring

Thought of the Day:
Einstein is considered a genius because of the theories he un-
covered. The reality is that he spent a lot of time concentrating
on a direction of thought and broke down the complicated questions into simple terms of understanding. This is the thought
process that should be used in studying for the finals. Break
down the assignments into a clear thought process.

From: Poppi
To: La Bella Verita
Sent: Spring

Thought of the Day:
The toughest thing to master is the proper allocation of your
resources. The most notable one is Time Management. The
use of time should be thought of in advance. Otherwise, valuable time that should have been spent wisely on a project will
be wasted.

From: Poppi
To: La Bella Verita
Sent: Spring

Thought of the Day:
College teaches you to Think and Problem Solve. The two main ingredients of Learning.

From: Poppi
To: La Bella Verita
Sent: Spring

Thought of the Day:
Last impressions are just as important as first impressions. When I have to do a presentation I want to be either first or last. By being first, I can set the standard for other firms to meet. By being last, I can leave the final impression on the decision makers.

From: Poppi
To: La Bella Verita
Sent: Spring

Thought of the Day:
Studying, just like work, can not be measured in the number of hours spent on a task. It has to be measured in the number of milestones it takes to achieve the task. It is two different mind sets: 1-I work 40 hours a week or 2-It will take me a week to achieve a certain level of a project development (40, 50 or more or less hours). It is more enjoyable to know you are proceeding to achieve a milestone than to dwell on minutes.

From: Poppi
To: La Bella Verita
Sent: Winter

Thought of the Day:
No one ever sat their way to success
Anonymous

From: Poppi
To: La Bella Verita
Sent: Winter

Thought of the Day:
A small stumble can prevent a big fall later in life.
English Proverb

From: Poppi
To: La Bella Verita
Sent: Autumn

Thought of the Day:
How could youths better learn to live than by once trying the
experiment of living. I think this would educate their minds as
much as math.
Thoreau

From: Poppi
To: La Bella Verita
Sent: Autumn

Did you see the president throw the first pitch out last night at
Yankees Stadium? The World Series is in full swing.
Did you know that there was another baseball game played last
night between the "Ghosts" and "Witches"? The witches lost because their "Bats" flew away.

Thought of the Day:
Hear the meaning within the word.
Shakespeare

From: Poppi
To: La Bella Verita
Sent: Spring

Thought of the Day:
The experience of "Being their Before", gives the confidence
needed to achieve the second time around.

From: Poppi
To: La Bella Verita
Sent: Spring

Here is a thought. The original is by Joe Paterno. I changed it a little because it was football related. It puts the college participation in sports experience in perspective.

Thought of the Day:
The purpose of college sports is to serve education, not the other way around. Ten years from now, student-athletes should be able to look back on college as a wonderful time of expanding themselves, not just four years of playing a specific sport.

From: Poppi
To: La Bella Verita
Sent: Spring

Thought of the Day:
Critical evaluation is important to improve, but it needs to be accepted and implemented in order to be effective.

From: Poppi
To: La Bella Verita
Sent: Spring

Thought of the Day:
Every success is usually an admission ticket to a new set of decisions.
Henry Kissinger

From: Poppi
To: La Bella Verita
Sent: Autumn

Thought of the Day:
In youth we learn, while in age we understand.
Ebner-Eschenbach

From: Poppi
To: La Bella Verita
Sent: Autumn

Thought of the Day:
The roots of education are bitter, but the fruit is sweet.
Aristotle

From: Poppi
To: La Bella Verita
Sent: Autumn

Thought of the Day:
Out of clutter, find simplicity
From discord, find harmony
In the middle of difficulty lies opportunity
Albert Einstein's three rules of work

From: Poppi
To: La Bella Verita
Sent: Autumn

Thought of the Day:
Intelligence without ambition is a bird without wings.
Danielson

From: Poppi
To: La Bella Verita
Sent: Autumn

Thought of the Day:
Success is simple arithmetic
Possibility = Reality...when you subtract "T" from CAN'T
Anonymous

From: Poppi
To: La Bella Verita
Sent: Autumn

Thought of the Day:
Knowledge is not information, it's transformation.
Osho

From: Poppi
To: La Bella Verita
Sent: Autumn

Thought of the Day:
A problem is a chance for you to do your best.
Duke Ellington

From: Poppi
To: La Bella Verita
Sent: Autumn

Thought of the Day:
Learn from yesterday, live for today, hope for tomorrow. The
important thing is to not stop questioning.
Albert Einstein

From: Poppi
To: La Bella Verita
Sent: Winter

Thought of the Day:
Problem solving is one main trait that you learn in college.
You learn it out of necessity
You master it by practicing responsibility.

From: Poppi
To: La Bella Verita
Sent: Winter

Thought of the Day:
Preparation is knowing ahead of time what is needed before starting a venture.

From: Poppi
To: La Bella Verita
Sent: Winter

Thought of the Day:
Besides learning to see, there is another art to be learned, not to see what is not.
Maria Mitchell

From: Poppi
To: La Bella Verita
Sent: Winter

Thought of the Day:
The person who makes no mistakes usually does not make anything.
Edward Phelps

From: Poppi
To: La Bella Verita
Sent: spring

The year is winding down. Both of you have grown. You both have had some successes and some failures.
Thought of the Day:
Don't let your success's get to your head, and don't take your failures to heart
Anonymous

Compete

7he NASA Associate Administrator (AA) for Education was a former Astronaut as well as a former National Football League (NFL) player. During the design phase of the renovated Education offices, we had a candid discussion on how do you redirect the focus from sports toward the sciences. This is especially hard if you have an audience of adolescent football players that only want to hear about playing in the NFL. The AA told the story how if you 1) know the geometry of the receiver route & 2) the speed (feet per second) by which the receiver runs & 3) the velocity by which the quarterback throws the ball; both quarterback & receiver will know the spot the ball & receiver should intersect. This builds confidence in the 2 players as well as the understanding that the opponent does not know this information and therefore, the team has a competitive edge. Science gives a team an advantage in the sports arena.

The majority of this chapter was inspired by sports competition. The Marymount University Women's Basketball team advanced to two Sweet 16's, an Elite 8 and a Final 4 in four straight years in the NCAA Division I I I Women's Basketball Tournament. The lady members of those teams had the same experience as teams that advanced in the NCAA Division I level. They excelled at their level of competition. That is exactly what competition does. It allows you to become the best that you can be, whether it is in the field of athletics, business or life in general.

From: Poppi
To: La Bella Verita
Sent: Autumn

The Olympics have some nice story lines about the athletes. Last night a USA swimmer won a Gold Metal, which is an accomplishment in itself. The story line is that the swimmer came from Russia (Ukraine) to the USA to have the opportunity to make a better life. He had to learn the language, went to school, worked 30 hours a week, and practiced swimming. He wanted to swim with the best and in return became the best.

This Olympic story is really no different than Great-Grand mom coming from Italy to have the opportunity to make a better life. She had to learn the language, worked more than 40 hours a week, raised 5 boys and became a pillar in her community.

Thought of the Day:
Everyone has an Olympic Dream

From: Poppi
To: La Bella Verita
Sent: Autumn

There was a swimmer that won a silver metal at the Olympics. He was deaf. He had to use a light to know when the starters horn went off. He could not hear the crowd cheering for him, but he could feel the electricity in the air.

Thought of the Day:
When on the journey to achievement, adaptation may be necessary to keep you on course.

From: Poppi
To: La Bella Verita
Sent: Autumn

Thought of the Day:
Competitive rivalry brings out the best in all participants.

From: Poppi
To: La Bella Verita
Sent: Autumn

The Olympics are over. There were some happy moments and some ugly displays of bad sportsmanship.

Thought of the Day:
Never complain, never taunt, never gloat. Respect the opponent for being in the competition.

From: Poppi
To: La Bella Verita
Sent: Autumn

Midnight Madness was a lot of fun. The campus was really rockin. The player introductions with the spotlights and music was really cool. The players really got into it. What a show.

Thought of the Day:
The applause that you receive is in appreciation for the preparation and effort given in competition. It is not for who you think you are (Ego or celebrity status)

From: Poppi
To: La Bella Verita
Sent: Autumn

You mentioned about the blisters on your feet because of the new team sneakers. Here is a little advice: Wear 2 pairs of socks, put Vaseline on the first pair on the areas that rub, place the second pair of socks over the first. The Vaseline will be between the socks. This should reduce the friction between the sneakers and the sensitive areas.

Thought of the Day:
One needs to be aware of the smallest detail in order to perform at your best.

From: Poppi
To: La Bella Verita
Sent: Autumn

The Penn State-Iowa football game was exciting, a double over-time thriller. Maybe you ladies can go next year to a game. I am reading about their coach, Joe Paterno. The book has a lot of thoughts and life experiences from a lifetime of coaching.

Thought of the Day:
The things that make a difference in a person's life are pride, loyalty and commitment.
Joe Paterno

From: Poppi
To: La Bella Verita
Sent: Autumn

I think you have a good team. There seems to be a nice friend-ship between the players. The next 4 months you will be spending a lot of time with these girls; practices, overnight trips to Boston & New York/New Jersey. They are your college sisters.

Thought of the Day:
The friendships that you make in college, both through the team and your major, will be friendships for a lifetime. You will feed off each others strengths in order to develop into independent productive adults. These friendships are different than the ones from high school. They are important in order to grow.

From: Poppi
To: La Bella Verita
Sent: Winter

Thought of the Day:
The true success of a sports program isn't in providing an overall winning record for the graduating senior class, but in the overall record of graduating seniors with "Class".

From: Poppi
To: La Bella Verita
Sent: Winter

Thought of the Day:
It is what you learn after you know it all that counts.
John Wooden

From: Poppi
To: La Bella Verita
Sent: Winter

Mom is exactly right. Everyone plays a role on a winning team.
Give 100% in practice and the team will be better. The talent at
this level is very good. Don't feel slighted, it is a team game and
you are an important part of it.

Thought of the Day:
Sometimes motherly advice is worth more than a college education.

From: Poppi
To: La Bella Verita
Sent: Winter

Thought of the Day:
Winners expect to win in advance. Life is a self-fulfilling proph-
ecy.
Anonymous

From: Poppi
To: La Bella Verita
Sent: Winter

Thought of the Day:
You can't achieve greatness unless you failed greatly.
Anonymous

From: Poppi
To: La Bella Verita
Sent: Winter

Huge win last night. You ladies need to play like that on the road in order to be a real championship team. Hopefully, the game in Baltimore this Saturday will be a good start.

Thought of the Day:
The diversity of the team is it's strength. Each player has a different story to tell with individual insight in approaching a situation. This opens up the mind for all.

From: Poppi
To: La Bella Verita
Sent: Winter

Thought of the Day:
Idolization is nothing more than hollow intimidation, while admiration builds solid inspiration.

From: Poppi
To: La Bella Verita
Sent: Winter

Thought of the Day:
The quality of a person's life is in direct proportion to their commitment to excellence, regardless of their chosen field of endeavour.
Vince Lombardi

From: Poppi
To: La Bella Verita
Sent: Winter

Thought of the Day:
Being in proper physical condition, combined with believing in oneself, provides the attitude to win; strength is shown outwardly while belief and confidence come from within.

From: Poppi
To: La Bella Verita
Sent: Spring

Congratulations on receiving an invitation to the NCAA Division III Women's Basketball Tournament. Just think, 5 years ago you were sitting on the bed crying because you got cut from the 8th grade team. One year ago you were playing in the Maryland State Championship and on Wednesday you will be on a team playing in the NCAA Tournament. Good Luck, but let's not loose focus and concentrate on your studies today.

Thought of the Day:
As David stood in front of Goliath, all he could focus on was that this giant of a man was the last obstacle in his quest for attaining his goal of being King.

From: Poppi
To: La Bella Verita
Sent: Spring

Thought of the Day:
Ability alone will not win the trophy. It takes focus, a confident mind and the proper attitude to move on.

From: Poppi
To: La Bella Verita
Sent: Spring

Thought of the Day:
Humankind has not woven the web of life. We are but one thread within it. Whatever we do to the web, we do to ourselves. All things are bound together.
Chief Seattle

From: Poppi
To: La Bella Verita
Sent: Spring

Congratulations on advancing to the NCAA Division I I I Sweet
16. Keep focus on your studies also. Don't let them slide.

Thought of the Day:
One needs to keep a "Sense of Balance" in their life to fully enjoy
the journey.

From: Poppi
To: La Bella Verita
Sent: Spring

Thought of the Day:
Too often we get distracted by what is outside our control. You
can't do anything about yesterday, you can do nothing about
tomorrow. It is yet to come. However, tomorrow is in large part
determined by what you do today. So, make today a master-
piece. You have control over that.
John Wooden

From: Poppi
To: La Bella Verita
Sent: Spring

Thought of the Day:
The most important thing in the Olympic games is not to win
but to take part, just as the most important thing in life is not to
triumph but in the struggle. The essential thing is not to have
conquered but to have fought well.
The Olympic Creed

From: Poppi
To: La Bella Verita
Sent: Spring

Thought of the Day:
The team on top of the mountain didn't fall there.
Written on Mom's coffee mug

From: Poppi
To: La Bella Verita
Sent: Autumn

This is a great e mail from Coach. It is not only reflective of sport, but also of life. The 3 "P" of proper Focus: Focus on the present, focus on the positive and focus on the process.

Thought of the Day:
I am not a teacher, but an awakener.
Robert Frost

From: Poppi
To: La Bella Verita
Sent: Winter

Thought of the Day:
How you handle a situation that is out of your control is a telling sign of Maturity. Awareness of the situation, adjustment and refocus will keep you in the "Competitive Life" game.

From: Poppi
To: La Bella Verita
Sent: Winter

Thought of the Day:
After climbing a great hill, one finds that there are many more hills to climb.
Nelson Mandala

From: Poppi
To: La Bella Verita
Sent: Autumn

Thought of the Day:
The repetition of the workouts give you a valuable lesson in "Appreciation of the Struggle". It is not fun to spend time on improving, but you get a little better each time. This is a lesson that carries over in Life. You get a certain appreciation out of the standard routine because you become better at what you do and eventually become a better person.

From: Poppi
To: La Bella Verita
Sent: Autumn

Thought of the Day:
The things that hurt, instruct.
Ben Franklin

From: Poppi
To: La Bella Verita
Sent: Autumn

Thought of the Day:
When things become routine, take it away and you will appreciate it more.

From: Poppi
To: La Bella Verita
Sent: Autumn

Thought of the Day:
Never let the fear of striking out get in your way.
Babe Ruth

From: Poppi
To: La Bella Verita
Sent: Autumn

Thought of the Day:
Action is eloquence.
Shakespeare

From: Poppi
To: La Bella Verita
Sent: Autumn

Thought of the Day:
Suffer now and live the rest of your life as a champion.
Muhammad Ali

From: Poppi
To: La Bella Verita
Sent: Autumn

So how was the Alumni game? Bonding with the retired players, huh?

Thought of the Day:

One of the advantages of college is that it establishes a life-long community of abundant opportunity. The alumni have been there. You have been handed a common relationship for access-ing their knowledge and thoughts. They have experience going though the system, being part of a successful team,competing on a high level and making their dream a reality. I am talking about LIFE, not sports.

From: Poppi
To: La Bella Verita
Sent: Autumn

Thought of the Day:

A positive experience in the arena of competition, erases all of the days of preparation that were filled with frustration and de-spair.

From: Poppi
To: La Bella Verita
Sent: Winter

Thought of the Day:

Throughout my life, I have always had the ability to concentrate on what has to be done and not worry about things I can't do anything about. If I can do something about it, I go after it and try to get it done by giving my best shot, If I succeed, fine, but if I fail, I put it behind me.
Joe Paterno

From: Poppi
To: La Bella Verita
Sent: Winter

Thought of the Day:

Unity (either team sports or in a business environment) is that added adrenaline needed to experience the joy of true accomplishment.

From: Poppi
To: La Bella Verita
Sent: Winter

Thought of the Day:

Be humble, keep focus and grind it out.
LaVar Arrington, Washington Redskin
(former Penn State linebacker, as if you couldn't see the Joe Paterno influence)

From: Poppi
To: La Bella Verita
Sent: Winter

Here is a story of a player from Washington DC. No colleges showed interest in him. He talked to his teacher who told him to go to Mount Saint Mary's for academics and forget about basketball. When he got there, he felt that he could probably be a walk on and he made it. This year as a senior, he is the starting point guard. But the interesting side of the story is his attitude. "I went there because of academics. I knew that academics was more important than basketball. I was a practice player and I wasn't frustrated. It was a challenge to earn playing time, I didn't get discouraged." His academic grades improved year after year and so did his playing time.

Thought of the Day:

Attitude is transferable and can give you confidence to achieve.

From: Poppi
To: La Bella Verita
Sent: Winter

I hope the team is focused for the game. There is no need to look too far ahead.

Thought of the Day:
The cart before the horse is neither beautiful nor useful
Henry David Thoreau

From: Poppi
To: La Bella Verita
Sent: Winter

Thought of the Day:
The real glory is being knocked to your knees and then coming back.
Vince Lombardi

From: Poppi
To: La Bella Verita
Sent: Winter

Thought of the Day:
Some people go through life pleased that the glass is half full. Others spend a lifetime lamenting that it's half-empty. The truth is: There is a glass with a certain volume of liquid in it. From there, it's up to you.
Dr. James S. Vuocolo

From: Poppi
To: La Bella Verita
Sent: Spring

Have a safe flight to Indiana. See you at the Final 4!

Thought of the Day:
Success is peace of mind obtained only through self-satisfaction in knowing you made the effort to do the best of which you're capable.
John Wooden

97

From: Poppi
To: La Bella Verita
Sent: Spring

Thought of the Day:
We're not all equal in talent. All we can do is make the most of
what we have and try to improve at all times.
John Wooden

From: Poppi
To: La Bella Verita
Sent: Spring

Thought of the Day:
Show me who you keep company with, and I'll tell you who you
are.
Muhammad Ali

From: Poppi
To: La Bella Verita
Sent: Spring

Thought of the Day:
A few numbers to ponder:
there are nationally 20,815 H.S. with 249,780 players
there are 1,028 colleges in the NCAA with 12,336 players
that means only 5% of H.S. players go on and play in college.
Out of 1,028 NCAA teams, (Division I, II & III) only:
48 teams experience the Sweet 16 or only 576 players
24 teams experience the Elite 8 or 288 players
12 teams experience the Final 4 or only 144 players.
That is only 1.2% of all NCAA players.

From: Poppi
To: La Bella Verita
Sent: Winter

Thought of the Day:
Every new day is an opportunity to raise the achievement bar
higher.

From: Poppi
To: La Bella Verita
Sent: Spring

That was one incredible weekend.....the NCAA Final 4. The experience of playing at the highest level of competition in the division is a lifetime achievement. You and the team gave a gutsy performance against the eventual National Champions. Congratulations on a fantastic season.

Thought of the Day:
Participating as an athlete in the NCAA Final 4 is more than a sports competition. The game is 1 part of the event. When asked about playing in the Final 4 it is the answer of the game becoming the event, and all the associated hoopla with it that people want to know about: the banquet, the press conferences, the autograph sessions, the media coverage, the send-off, the airplane trip, etc. The positive experience of the event is the lifetime memory, because stripped of the event......it was just a GAME.

From: Poppi
To: La Bella Verita
Sent: Autumn

Thought of the Day:
Every once in awhile you see yourself in a player.
Pat Summit

From: Poppi
To: La Bella Verita
Sent: Spring

Thought of the Day:
The time will come for every athlete to take the uniform off for the last time. You can walk away from the court, but you can't walk away from the game. Fulfillment is knowing that the game gave back to you life lessons which made you a better person.... and because of that, the game is part of you forever.

Create

One day, while inspecting the contractor's punch list (items needed to be completed prior to final release of payment), I noticed a scientist sitting in the Galley (renovated breakroom) staring at the freshly painted blank wall. I asked if there is a concern with the wall finish or color. The scientist said that the Chief NASA Scientist has asked her to use the blank wall as a canvas. Confused, I asked her to please expand on her statement. She showed me her office and on the walls were beautiful paintings of distant planets, Mars and the moon. She told the story of how there were two professions that she wanted to be when she was a little girl; an artist and an astronaut. Her dream of being an astronaut was shattered when she found out that at that time, women were not allowed to be astronauts. Later in her life, a professor suggested that she take a look into Planetary Science. The professor explained that you can hold in your hand a moon rock, study the scientific components and know that you are touching an object from a distant place and time. This instilled the passion to become one of NASA's top Planetary Scientists. Her artistic ability allows the transfer of that passion onto canvas.

Appreciation in the beauty of aesthetics. The very nature of being creative means that timeless inspiration can strike seemingly at anytime. Being creative makes a person's uniqueness shine. Creativity is "Thinking outside the Box".

Business Computing World defines Creativity as the ability to visualize connections between pieces of information and translate those connections into innovative products, services or ideas. Being creative makes a person valuable to an organization.

From: Poppi
To: La Bella Verita
Sent: Winter

Thought of the Day:
There are lessons that can be learned through the Beauty of Nature

From: Poppi
To: La Bella Verita
Sent: Winter

Thought of the Day:
Traditional Music seems to put a "Calm" in everyone that listens to it with open ears.

From: Poppi
To: La Bella Verita
Sent: Spring

Thought of the Day:
It is the internal experience of ourselves in "The Moment" that leaves a long-lasting imprint on our psyche.
Dr. Harvey L. Rich

From: Poppi
To: La Bella Verita
Sent: Spring

Thought of the Day:
A little humor breaks the tension of a stressful situation. So every once in awhile.....SMILE.

From: Poppi
To: La Bella Verita
Sent: Autumn

Thought of the Day:
I find that if you clear your mind from problems or stress for a few hours and get a good-relaxed nights sleep, you awake with creative ideas and solutions to the problems.

From: Poppi
To: La Bella Verita
Sent: Autumn

Thought of the Day:
You can complain because roses have thorns, or you can rejoice because thorns have roses.
Ziggy (the comic strip....yeah, that's right!)

From: Poppi
To: La Bella Verita
Sent: Autumn

Thought of the Day:
All Youth are gifted, some just open their packages earlier than others.
Michael Cain

From: Poppi
To: La Bella Verita
Sent: Winter

Have a better day than yesterday.
Thought of the Day:
If there were never any clouds, how could we ever appreciate the sun?
Anonymous

From: Poppi
To: La Bella Verita
Sent: Winter

Thought of the Day:
Appreciation works in both directions.

From: Poppi
To: La Bella Verita
Sent: Spring

Thought of the Day:
To make a wish come true, whisper it to a butterfly.
Indian Legend

From: Poppi
To: La Bella Verita
Sent: Spring

It is suppose to be 90 degrees again today, so it is time for the
Hawaiian Shirt!

Thought of the Day:
There are people that need to dress in the latest fashion to be
needed....and there are people who are fashionable. The difference is not in the clothes but in the attitude of the person wearing the clothes.

From: Poppi
To: La Bella Verita
Sent: Spring

Thought of the Day:
Learn some and Think some and Draw some and Paint and
Sing and Dance and Play everyday some.
Robert Fulghum

From: Poppi
To: La Bella Verita
Sent: Autumn

Did you see the Telethon to raise money for the victims of the
9-11 tragedy? The artists that performed were all good. Except
for a few songs that dealt with "Let's all just get along and live
in peace", the songs were moving and appropriate. I just think
songs about Utopia are not appropriate in a time of Mourning.
There is time in the future for that type of message. WE don't
need "Peaceniks" right now, but "People of Comfort".

Thought of the Day:
There is a clear difference between Artists and Entertainers.
Artists (Musicians, etc.) capture an individual's emotion in or-
ganized sound that can be brought back to the surface at any
moment. Entertainers only capture a group's moment in time.
One is for inner contemplation while the other is for inner escape.

From: Poppi
To: La Bella Verita
Sent: Autumn

Too bad you won't be able to see Uncle D. when he comes to
Washington D.C. He usually stays at the hotel across from the
Watergate. You know, the one from President Nixon fame where
the break in of the Democratic Headquarters cost the presi-
dency....oh yeah, that's right, I was the one in college back then!
Anyway, the Kennedy Center show that he is involved with is
only a few days long. It is suppose to be a really creative type of
dance. Than he heads back to New York City I guess.

Thought of the Day:
"Vision" is the Art of seeing Imagination.
Anonymous

From: Poppi
To: La Bella Verita
Sent: Autumn

One of the Beatle's, George Harrison, the quiet one (that is how he became to be known), passed away this morning. He had cancer. The Beatle's were way before your time, but their influence in popular music has been profound. They were true artists. They were the interpreters of the day through their organized sound (music). George Harrison's songs always had a spiritual and timeless theme to them. Even Frank Sinatra recorded one of them. The name of the song is "Something".

Thought of the Day:

George Harrison, was known as the "Quiet Beatle". He developed his music in privacy. He was at peace and comfortable with himself when writing his music as reflected in his recordings. Those recordings give everyone a sense of inner peace, and as such, are timeless and not trendy or nostalgic. One theme throughout his music is reflecting on the "Higher Order" (sense of the Divine). Listen to it and you will hear it. So, when things seem like they are going in the wrong direction, just think of a line from one of his songs:

It's Alright.......Here comes the Sun.

The Framework
for Living

Relationships
Vocation
and Freedom

Relationships

The Space Shuttle program completed it's final mission on July 21, 2011. NASA commissioned a medallion to commemorate the 30 year program. Each medallion contains metal flown on one of the Space Shuttle missions. The back has an inscription that honors the participants, who interacted at all levels of the mission. The inscription reads, "Excellence achieved by those who believed." Thousands of professional relationships were developed, nurtured and tested through success and tragedy over a three decade span to make the Space Shuttle program a success.

Dr. Orv Owens is a world renowned motivational speaker. His teachings are based on developing relationships. I was honored when Dr. Owens commissioned me to design his Conference Center on the Florida West Coast. We developed the design program to create a natural environment to enhance the four "Relationships of Life" that are key to his teachings. The four relationships are critical in having a fulfilled life. This chapter is divided into "Thoughts of the Day" that are based on the four "Relationships of Life". The easiest to achieve is the Outward (being friendly with people)and Downward (how you are perceived by the younger generation or subordinates). The more difficult to achieve is the Upward (whom you have a responsibility of reporting to and the higher order) and the Inward (being comfortable with yourself).

Inward

From: Poppi
To: La Bella Verita
Sent: Autumn

Thought of the Day:
Home is now any environment that encloses the "Real Person".

From: Poppi
To: La Bella Verita
Sent: Spring

Nice weekend. Did anybody get downtown to see the Cherry Blossoms?

Thought of the Day:
Spring is a time for renewal. Every year the cherry blossoms bloom and every year people look at them in awe, like they will never see them again. This is the feeling of renewing oneself.

From: Poppi
To: La Bella Verita
Sent: Spring

Thought of the Day:
Don't permit fear of failure to prevent effort. We are all imperfect and will fail on occasions, but fear of failure is the greatest failure of all.
John Wooden

From: Poppi
To: La Bella Verita
Sent: Spring

Thought of the Day:
Spring is a time for renewal. Renewing your faith, family ties, friendships with people and most of all renewing your belief in yourself.

From: Poppi
To: La Bella Verita
Sent: Winter

Thought of the Day:
Happiness is not a goal in life to achieve, but is an everyday
way of life.

From: Poppi
To: La Bella Verita
Sent: Winter

Thought of the Day:
The highest reward for a person's toil is not what they get for it,
but what they become by it.
Ruskin

From: Poppi
To: La Bella Verita
Sent: Autumn

Thought of the Day:
To see the world, you must close your eyes.
Anonymous

From: Poppi
To: La Bella Verita
Sent: Autumn

Thought of the Day:
Do not be tricked into believing that modern decor must be
slick or psychedelic or natural or modern art or plants or anything else current taste-makers claim. It is most beautiful when
it comes straight from your life.......the things you care for, the
things that tell your story.
Christopher Alexander

From: Poppi
To: La Bella Verita
Sent: Winter

Thought of the Day:
If you smile when no one else is around, you really mean it.
Andy Rooney

From: Poppi
To: La Bella Verita
Sent: Winter

Thought of the Day:
Light the Fire Within
Winter Olympic Theme

From: Poppi
To: La Bella Verita
Sent: Autumn

Thought of the Day:
Sometimes when you hit a dead end, a little adjustment will start you moving again. If things look IMPOSSIBLE, a little adjustment will show that I'M POSSIBLE.

From: Poppi
To: La Bella Verita
Sent: Winter

Thought of the Day:
Peace is found not in what surrounds us, but is what we hold within.
Poster in a "Successories" retail store.

From: Poppi
To: La Bella Verita
Sent: Spring

Thought of the Day:
The greatest worth of a person is being oneself.

From: Poppi
To: La Bella Verita
Sent: Winter

Thought of the Day:
People become really quite remarkable when they start thinking that they can do things. When they believe in themselves they have the first secret of success.
Norman Vincent Peale

From: Poppi
To: La Bella Verita
Sent: Autumn

Thought of the Day:
To grow externally, we must grow internally.
Anonymous

From: Poppi
To: La Bella Verita
Sent: Winter

Thought of the Day:
It is important to not only develop the physical self but also the inner self. The physical self is what people see, but the inner self is what people feel.

From: Poppi
To: La Bella Verita
Sent: Autumn

Thought of the Day:
Our lives improve when we take chances...and the first and most difficult risk we can take is to be honest with ourselves.
Walter Anderson

Outward

From: Poppi
To: La Bella Verita
Sent: Winter

Thought of the Day:
Light tomorrow with today
Browning

From: Poppi
To: La Bella Verita
Sent: Winter

Thought of the Day:
Once in awhile, take time to Smile.

From: Poppi
To: La Bella Verita
Sent: Spring

Thought of the Day:
The more concerned we become over the things we can't control, the less we will do with the things we can control.
John Wooden

From: Poppi
To: La Bella Verita
Sent: Spring

Thought of the Day:
Today's weather forecast calls for it to be a rainy day...but today's outlook is sunny.

From: Poppi
To: La Bella Verita
Sent: Autumn

Thought of the Day:
Think for yourself and let others enjoy the privilege of doing so too.
Voltaire

From: Poppi
To: La Bella Verita
Sent: Autumn

Mom & I went to the concert on the beach...it was fun. I was thinking that the whole environment was so pleasant for this type of concert...the beach, stage right next to the ocean, the festive atmosphere of the people.

Thought of the Day:
The creation of the environment can cause an effect on a person,which could be projected outward as a negative or positive response.

From: Poppi
To: La Bella Verita
Sent: Spring

One of the things, as you are currently learning in life, is to develop relationships. They can develop in either direction; positive or negative. But, in order to learn something from relating with people is to listen to criticism. Only you can decide to accept or reject it.

Thought of the Day:
The avoid criticism; do nothing, say nothing, BE NOTHING.
Elbert Hubbard

Downward

From: Poppi
To: La Bella Verita
Sent: Spring

Thought of the Day:
Toward the end of the Civil War, reparations were being dis-
cussed in the White House. One of the advisors told Lincoln that
he favored punishing the South. Lincoln said no. The advisor
said "Mr. President, you're suppose to destroy your enemies,
not make friends of them." Lincoln replied, "Am I not destroying
an enemy when I make a friend of him?"

From: Poppi
To: La Bella Verita
Sent: Spring

Thought of the Day:
There are 4 fears to overcome in order to have healthy relationships with people: Fear of Failure, Fear of Loss of Power, Fear
of the Unknown and Fear of Thoughts about You.
Dr. Orv Owens

From: Poppi
To: La Bella Verita
Sent: Spring

Thought of the Day:
Be most interested in finding the Best Way", not in having your
"Own Way".

From: Poppi
To: La Bella Verita
Sent: Autumn

Thought of the Day:
Be kind, for everyone you meet is fighting a harder battle.

From: Poppi
To: La Bella Verita
Sent: Winter

Thought of the Day:
Do not expect to accomplish your dreams if you're not willing to help others accomplish their's.
Kaughee Vill

From: Poppi
To: La Bella Verita
Sent: Winter

Thought of the Day:
It's important that we learn to use all our strength. This includes inner resources such as discipline, courage and even love. But it also includes outer resources. Just as we should be willing to help others we should be willing to ask the help of others. It's one of the great things about being human.
Coach Bill Finney

From: Poppi
To: La Bella Verita
Sent: Winter

Thought of the Day:
You never know when someone will catch a Dream from you. You never know when that little word or something you do opens the windows of the mind that seeks the Light. The way you live doesn't matter at all...BUT IT MIGHT. So, just in case, it could be that another's life through you might possibly change for the better, with a broader and brighter view. It seems it might be worth a try at pointing the way to the right...of course it may not matter at all...BUT IT MIGHT.
Anonymous

Upward

From: Poppi
To: La Bella Verita
Sent: Winter

Thought of the Day:
You can't help someone get up a hill without getting closer to the top yourself.
General Norman Scharzkopf

From: Poppi
To: La Bella Verita
Sent: Autumn

Thought of the Day:
Be careful that the toes you step on today...are not connected to the butt you must kiss tomorrow.
Anonymous

From: Poppi
To: La Bella Verita
Sent: Winter

Thought of the Day:
You both made the best of opportunities that were in front of you. You made the decision to pursue the opportunity, but remember that it had to be offered up in the first place. So, be thankful to the people or organization that allowed the opportunity to surface.

From: Poppi
To: La Bella Verita
Sent: Spring

This is what happens when you reach a certain Plateau of Achievement. People take notice and want to know more about the experience. They want to know what the Final 4 was like, how you got there, not the games that you won but also the preparation. They want to know you as a person.

Thought of the Day:
People, especially children, take notice when a person reaches a Plateau of Achievement. They look up to you to see what they are suppose to be...let's not disappoint them.

From: Poppi
To: La Bella Verita
Sent: Spring

Thought of the Day:
Upperclassmen provide the Guiding Leadership for the Team. They give their best effort for their abilities. They have the character to treat opponents with respect. They know that there is a lesson learned from each contest. They provide the best example for the underclassmen to follow.

From: Poppi
To: La Bella Verita
Sent: Autumn

Thought of the Day:
What I do you can not do; but what you do, I can not do. The needs are great, and none of us, including me, ever do great things. But we can all do small things, with great love and to-gether we can do something wonderful.
Mother Teresa

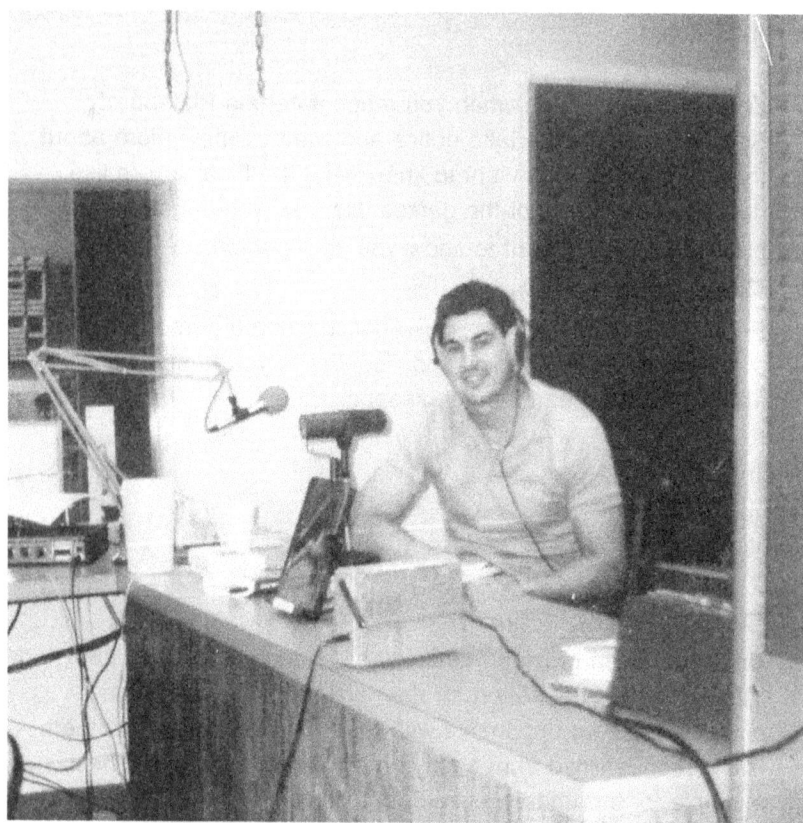

Vocation

Fulfillment is being comfortable in your daily events, which includes making a living. Whatever you choose, have enjoyment in the time spent working for your livelihood. Take Pride in the daily work. Be confident in the decisions that you make in pursuing your life's work. Weigh daily decisions based on the Right-Wrong Value judgements that were passed down to you by your family and cherish the relationships that have been developed along life's journey. One day, someone will look up to you and admire your achievements. The daily routine builds character, persistence and is the basis of personal wealth.

From: Poppi
To: La Bella Verita
Sent: Winter

Thought of the Day:
A monetary transaction is the last item to do in a well thought out plan. Commitment of all parties is the first.

From: Poppi
To: La Bella Verita
Sent: Autumn

Thought of the Day:
When I grow up, I want to be a little boy.
Joseph Heller

From: Poppi
To: La Bella Verita
Sent: Autumn

Thought of the Day:
Behold the Turtle. He only makes progress when he sticks his neck out.
James Bryant Covant

From: Poppi
To: La Bella Verita
Sent: Autumn

Thought of the Day:
The secret of success is consistency of purpose.
Disraeli

From: Poppi
To: La Bella Verita
Sent: Winter

Thought of the Day:
Doing one's best is the highest reward.

From: Poppi
To: La Bella Verita
Sent: Spring

Thought of the Day:
The American Dream is about hard work and determination.
These are the ingredients to realize your dream.
K. Baker

From: Poppi
To: La Bella Verita
Sent: Spring

Thought of the Day:
Those that are happy, don't always have the best, but make the
best of what they have.
Anonymous

From: Poppi
To: La Bella Verita
Sent: Spring

Thought of the Day:
Life doesn't have to be perfect to be wonderful.
Anonymous

From: Poppi
To: La Bella Verita
Sent: Spring

Thought of the Day:
The only way to have a life is to commit to it like crazy.
Angelina Jolie
(Her father is Jon Voight, a Catholic University of America
graduate)

From: Poppi
To: La Bella Verita
Sent: Autumn

Thought of the Day:
Life's challenges are not supposed to paralyze you. They're
supposed to help discover who you are.
Bernice Johnson Reagan

From: Poppi
To: La Bella Verita
Sent: Autumn

Thought of the Day:
Whatever you decide to pursue, always strive for perfection. If
you do not strive for excellence, you will achieve only mediocrity.
You can never achieve perfection, but if you strive for perfection,
you can achieve excellence.
Gisler

From: Poppi
To: La Bella Verita
Sent: Autumn

Thought of the Day:
Not achieving something that is a high priority in your life does
not mean that it is not attainable. Circumstances may dictate
an adjustment may be needed on the path taken or the level of
achievement. Wisdom will guide you in the proper direction or
you will develop a jealous contempt for not achieving your goal.

From: Poppi
To: La Bella Verita
Sent: Autumn

Thought of the Day:
Relaxed confidence in the task at hand builds inner support.

Freedom

he day was the anniversary of September 11th, the attack on America. I was having lunch with three exchange students from Argentina. They were in their last semester of Architectural studies in the Graduate School at Virginia Tech. The discussion focused on the World Trade Center Memorial Proposal that was hanging on my office wall. The first few minutes were spent on the events of that day. The remaining time was spent on what does it mean to be in America and the freedom of opportunities she provides. They were not impressed by America, but rather inspired by her. I asked them what is the biggest lesson that they learned while studying here. They replied "There is a timely struggle with every choice, but the lessons learned are timeless. Only in America we are provided with the opportunity to choose the right struggle." Their last graduate school project before heading home to Argentina was a 3D video interpretation of the WTC Memorial Proposal that was hanging on my office wall. The illustration on the opposite page is a frame from that video.

Freedom is knowing that the world will protect your decisions of risk taking, ownership of personal property, artistic works, items of purchase or even payment for a service rendered, as long as the action is honorable. Freedom is knowing that the world that you enjoy will be protected.

From: Poppi
To: La Bella Verita
Sent: Autumn

Thought of the Day:
Independence rests on the foundation of responsibility.

From: Poppi
To: La Bella Verita
Sent: Autumn

I get news reports e mailed to me from the New York Times each morning. It is kind of neat because they keep me up to date on what is happening. This morning I opened an article from the "This day in history" section from September 17, 1862. It is about the battle of Antetiem. It is an interesting article, especially living down the road from where the battle took place. The battle was the one with the most lose of life in the Civil War. One of the reasons was the tactics that the southern forces (the New York Times refers to them as rebels) used during the battle. They would unfurl a Union flag and would wave it as the Union forces approached. Therefore, the Union forces would think that they were friendly soldiers and put down their weapons. The rebels would open fire on them. This is a historical lesson in deception. Maybe people should read an article from "This day in history" before they read today's headlines. It makes you think if a lesson has been learned or is history about to be repeated. The head-line today deals with the world conflict with Iraq.

Thought of the Day:
All the reasons for attack have been eliminated.
Iraqi Deputy Minister Taraq Aziz

From: Poppi
To: La Bella Verita
Sent: Autumn

Thought of the Day:
The most valuable of all talents is that of never using two words when one will do.
Thomas Jefferson

From: Poppi
To: La Bella Verita
Sent: Autumn

Thought of the Day:
As the winds from Hurricane Isabel swept over Arlington National Cemetery, the soldiers who guard the Tomb of the Unknowns
were given for the first time in history, permission to abandon
their posts and seek shelter. "That's not going to happen", said
Sgt. Holmes, standing vigil on overnight duty. "It's just considered to be the greatest honor to go out there and guard. It's
not only the unknowns, it's a symbol that represents everyone
who's fought and died for our country."

From: Poppi
To: La Bella Verita
Sent: Spring

I know you ladies have been busy, but take a minute and view
the news once in awhile. There was a recall vote in California to
replace the Governor, something pretty rare. Arnold Shwarzen-
negger, an immigrant from Austria, who came here in 1968 with
$20.00 in his pocket, is now the Governor. He came here with
Dreams; of being a Mr. Olympia bodybuilder, a movie actor, a
successful businessman & philanthropist.

Thought of the Day:
Every once in awhile, people go into the voting booth and Vote
their Dreams.

From: Poppi
To: La Bella Verita
Sent: Autumn

There is a very disturbing situation that deals with Bioethics and
human life taking place in Florida. Is this where the American
future is heading?

Thought of the Day:
It is TRUE that a nation is judged by the way it treats it's most
vulnerable citizens.
Wesley Smith   129

From: Poppi
To: La Bella Verita
Sent: Autumn

Thought of the Day:
One man with courage is a majority.
Andrew Jackson

From: Poppi
To: La Bella Verita
Sent: Autumn

Thought of the Day:
One ought never to turn one's back on a threatened danger and
try to run away from it. If you do that, you will double the danger.
But if you meet it promptly and without flinching, you will reduce
the danger by half. Never run away from anything. NEVER!
Winston Churchill

From: Poppi
To: La Bella Verita
Sent: Autumn

Thought of the Day:
Casting your ballot for president gives a sense of pride.

From: Poppi
To: La Bella Verita
Sent: Autumn

Thought of the Day:
The common man's vote is the most powerful decision that this
country has. It does not matter if you are rich or poor, intelligent
or uneducated, each vote cast has the same value. It is the
american voice.

From: Poppi
To: La Bella Verita
Sent: Autumn

Thought of the Day:
The concept of "Truth" has one rule. That rule is "A is A", not "A is B or C, but A". The truth is the truth and no matter how long it takes the truth will prevail.

From: Poppi
To: La Bella Verita
Sent: Autumn

Thought of the Day:
He who deceives, will find those who let themselves be deceived.
Machiavelli

From: Poppi
To: La Bella Verita
Sent: Winter

We now have a new president. His inauguration speech was uplifting. He has some ideas and an agenda that he wants to accomplish. I hope the country wishes him well.

Thought of the Day:
There is one thing stronger than all the armies in the world, and that is an idea whose time has come.
Victor Hugo

Conclusion

Olympian Bob Richards is credited for saying, "God must have really loved ordinary people because he made so many of them...and everyday ordinary people get up and do extraordinary things."

The General Services Administration (GSA) gave NASA the directive that the renovation had to meet the level of the United States Green Building Council (USGBC) Leadership in Energy & Environmental Design (LEED) Silver Certification. The renovation achieved the LEED Gold Certification. This sustainability achievement as well as providing a completely redesigned infrastructure while maintaining occupancy & headquarters operations, the renovation team was awarded the NASA Agency Group Achievement Award. This award is usually handed out to teams of rocket scientists or engineers who develop state of the art technologies or discover new worlds. After receiving the award by the Administrator, it was time for my last walk down the Great Hall to exit the facility.

Every month at NASA Headquarters, a new presentation is displayed on the Great Hall wall. The last presentation before my departure was on the Origins of the Universe. This was a fascinating display and provoked a number of questions. I was lucky to have the opportunity to discuss the display with one of NASA's historians. The historian noted that the presentation does not settle any science on the Origin of the Universe. It is impossible, because there are too many unanswered questions. The Big Bang is a theory, but there are other theories being tested. One theory suggests that the age of the universe could be infinite. This theory, if probable, could explain what "Dark Matter", the mysterious substance that makes up the majority of matter in the universe is actually made of. Another question is, can the theory that life evolved from a single cell be verified? Evolution can explain how animals evolve through time, but can't verify the true beginning, at least, with the present knowledge of the human mind. It is our quest for discovering the truth that keeps humans looking for the answers.

I was fortunate to be in the audience of presentations by world renowned scientists. The most important lesson I took away from this experience is to "Question". The answer today maybe outside our human capacity, but maybe not in the future.

In conclusion, human beings are flawed, which in turn make human institutions flawed. Mistakes will always be made and corrected. The human race is forgiving and will always want the best for everyone.

Carly Fiorina, former chairman & CEO of Hewlett-Packard, said that "No one of us is any better than any other one of us. Everyone has gifts, everyone wants to live a life of dignity, of purpose and of meaning, and everyone can do that."

Do what you can to make the world a better place when you entered, by pursuing your dream and passing down life's lessons along the way.

This simple task is what makes a simple ordinary person, extraordinary.

Thank You for taking the time to reflect on these simple thoughts.

John Ferri

The Next Step
Antonio Drej Project

The Antonio Drej Project is YOUR project. The project is envisioned to be a collection of inspirational thoughts and quotes from everyday people, from all walks of life. Preferably, people belonging to the "Baby Boom Generation" (1946-1964) or older. Anyone from this generation or older, generally has the integrity and wisdom to pass down to "La Bella Verita". The collection will be assembled into both paperback and Kindle e reader format for distribution in the United States as well as overseas.

Go to www.CIPubHouse.com for information on how to participate.

Acknowledgements

First I would like to acknowledge the Holy Spirit for providing guidance throughout each day. I would like to thank my wife, Christie, for giving support to finish this project. I would like to acknowledge my daughters, Angelina and Nikki for without them the e mails would have never been written. I would like to acknowledge my grandchildren, Carmella and Luca San Severino, for providing the inspiration to start this project. I would like to acknowledge family and friends for providing the insight for interpreting life's simple events. I would like to acknowledge mentors, NASA personnel and people who have influenced and inspired me along my life's journey. I would like to acknowledge the professional personnel who without their expertise this book could not have been published.

Photographs

Front Cover
Standing on the NASA Headquarters Roof Top Terrace

Dream
Dreaming of Christmas in New Market, Maryland.

Day of Trepidation
Standing in front of the New York New York resort in Las Vegas, Nevada on September 11, 2005

Faith
St. Patrick's Cathedral in New York City

Family
Family Easter Dinner circa 1964

Values
A quiet morning on the dock with Grand pop & Angelina in Bethany Beach, Delaware.

Learn
Nikki graduating college.

Compete
Angelina shooting a 3 pointer for the Final Four bound Marymount University Saints.

Create
Central Atrium of the Guggenheim Museum

Relationships
Great Grand Mom, Grand Mom and Nanni during the holidays.

Vocation
Cohost of The Home Show; a weekly residential architecture show on WMET, 1150 AM in Washington DC. circa mid 1990's

Freedom
Illustration from World Trade Center Memorial Proposal # 790373

Conclusion
World Trade Center Memorial